WHAT TO DO ABOUT SCHOOL

Jyoti Imix

Jyoti Imix spent 10 years travelling the world as an adventurer and academic researcher, searching for clues about how to reform the education system. She is a passionate children's rights activist and has worked with young people in a variety of settings, from third sector organisations to alternative schools. When she's not writing, geeking out, influencing or on the road, you'll find her barefoot and up a tree somewhere in Yorkshire.

WHAT TO DO ABOUT SCHOOL

Making Space for Children's Learning, Development, Authenticity and Autonomy

Jyoti Imix

I feel in this time... it is a necessity to have a plan, a manifesto, an alternative. It's a question of life and death for our species... after tragedies one has to invent a new world, knit it or embroider, make it up. It's not gonna be given to you because you deserve it, it doesn't work that way. You have to imagine something that doesn't exist and dig a cave into the future and demand space. It's a territorial hope affair... in the future it will become your reality.

Bjork

This book is dedicated to lots of people.

My mum, who taught me the importance of heart seeds and their impact. My grandad, who pushed me to utilise my potential and see how necessary it is to get as big as we can. Fraser, who always believed in me no matter how many times I dropped out. Sue, without whom this book would not exist. Zach, my cousin and copywriter. And all the amazing people, big and little, that I met during my research adventures at Rock Tree Sky and The Open School.

Mainly, though, this book is dedicated to children. May we respect them, listen to them, learn from them and create the space they deserve to occupy in this world.

Copyright © 2022 Jyoti Imix
All rights reserved.
Cover design by Jyoti Imix
Book design by Jyoti Imix
No part of this book can be reproduced in any form or by written, electronic or mechanical, including photocopying, recording, or by any information retrieval system without written permission in writing by the author.
Self-Published
Printed by Book Printing UK www.bookprintinguk.com
Remus House, Coltsfoot Drive, Peterborough, PE2 9BF
Printed in Great Britain
Although every precaution has been taken in the preparation of this book, the publisher and author assume no responsibility for errors or omissions. Neither is any liability assumed for damages resulting from the use of information contained herein.
ISBN 978-1-3999-3226-4

CONTENTS

SETTING THE SCENE 10

PART 1 17
WHAT *IS* CHILDHOOD? 18
   Why Kids Can't Be Free 22
PLAY 30
   The Awesomeness That is Playwork 34
   Risk 36
   Play to Heal 39
THE FOOLIN' OF SCHOOLIN' 44
   A Little History 45
   This is How You Memorise 46
   Seriously Important Subjects (100 Years Ago) 49
   The Curriculum Behind the Curtain 53
   You (Don't) Got the Power! 57
   Prove Yourself 59
   Who's the Best? 61
   Where the Life Skills at? 62
   The Free Babysitter 63
   TRY Harder 65
   Big Business 67
WORMHOLES AND THE QUANTUM WORLD 70

PART 2 77
RUDOLF STEINER 78
   Steiner/Waldorf Schools 85
KRISHNAMURTI 92

Krishnamurti Schools **94**
MONTESSORI SCHOOLS **97**
    Classroom/Research Lab 98
GREEN SCHOOL BALI **101**
    Project-Based Learning 102
    Intentional Space 105
SUMMERHILL **110**
    Democratic Education 112

PART 3 119
THE BACKDROP **120**
    Class and Socio-Economic Status 120
    Being a Researcher 124
    Home Education 126
    Self-Directed Learning and Unschooling 129

THE RESEARCH BEGINS 135
THE ENVIRONMENT **138**
    Space Ownership 139
    The Politics of Space 143
    Permission 147
    Nature 149
THE MENTORS **152**
    Self-Awareness & Role Modelling 153
    The Perspective of the Child 155
    The Adult Role 158
CHILDREN'S CULTURE **164**
    Risk 166
    Gaming 168
    Gender and Sexuality 175
    Queering the Norm 181

Sex 184
  Race 189
NEURODIVERSITY **192**
  ADHD 192
  Autism 197
ORGANISATION **201**
  Decision Making 202
  Meeting Tools 205
  Structure and Flow 207
  Conflict Resolution 209
  Emotional Processing 212
PARENTAL INVOLVEMENT **218**
PROGRESSION **221**

MAKING THE LEAP 226
GRASSROOTS COLLABORATION **227**

CONCLUDING THOUGHTS 230
MY PART IN THE SHIFT **232**

ACE STUFF I READ/WATCHED 242
I recommend these: **242**
  Books 242
  Documentaries 243
  Websites 244
More books (if you wanna geek out): **244**

SETTING THE SCENE

As I begin to write from my cosy little home in the UK, there is a global crisis outside my window. The world that existed before 2019 is gone and we have space for change, perhaps for the first time in generations. This book exists to support grassroots education reform and the timing could not be more relevant.

When thinking about restructuring society to align with greater harmony, my focus is and always has been on the reformation of the schooling system. Small humans spend most of their time at school; it is a pivotal piece of our collective messy puzzle, as a cause of distortion or a potential space to remedy it. Children need us. They've outgrown what's on offer educationally (I'm yet to be convinced that it ever fit) and people working in mainstream schools are often so overstretched that it's rare to find teachers with the capacity or bandwidth to champion change, even if they feel it in their hearts.

I feel the mission of the moment is about all of us making different choices in our microenvironments instead of pleading with governments to change things on our behalf. Activism doesn't simply mean protesting; it is about conscious action for a cause. This could be something simple that we do in our home or it may be birthing a project; it will look different for each one of us. The truth is, though, we all have a responsibility. Children don't have a collective voice or the power to make noise about what is affecting them and, in the same way as with the environment and the animals we share the planet with; it's down to grown-ups to be advocates, to speak up and create change on their behalf.

I've had the privilege to visit many continents and meet many flavours of human being. My nomadic adventures always mysteriously led me back to the topic of this book (make of that what you wish!). The happiest people I've met lived in third world countries. They weren't formally educated, had very few possessions and had a richness in their eyes I've not found anywhere else. In the west, despite the fact that most go through school and have jobs which create some kind of 'stability' in their lives, people are plagued with depression and repeated experiences of existential crisis. Our carrot chasing has not led to fulfilment; for many it has led to a serious case of 'what's the point...?' and, 'who even am I?!'

We built our education system and our world upon the notion that we need to be purposely programmed and moulded to grow into the best version of ourselves. My work as a therapist, educator and indeed my own experience as a human suggest that the opposite is in fact the case. When we strip all the forced learning and experience back, something intrinsic takes hold and seems to guide us toward growth and development. When we let the innate drive of our curiosity and passion lead, we develop in remarkable ways. This is beautifully illustrated when children learn to walk. As soon as they are ready the instinctive drive switches on and through a process of trial, error and sheer determination, the child begins to walk on their own. Parents don't attend 'preparation to teach walking' classes; they facilitate the process, hopefully with a whole lot of love and encouragement. But even if that is lacking, children figure it out themselves. Perhaps babies are also inspired by the upright humans around them but regardless of how the drive works, I feel that this demonstrates our ability to work things out. We are not driving the evolution train, no matter what our minds and forefathers might like to suggest; we're passengers.

What if we were to allow and trust this drive to lead life? In the same way that we ensure children don't bash their faces on the coffee table as they attempt to stand up for the first time, maybe our role in the development process is about creating safe, loving and inspirational spaces for the internal facilities of human-beingness to be in charge. Y'know, the drive that keeps our heart beating and makes us breathe in and out without thinking - the one that actually keeps us alive?

This ideal may seem far-fetched right now. But come with me on a journey to deconstruct the ideas we hold to be true and let's see where we end up.

I'm a playworker, academic researcher, activist and deeply spiritual human so expect the reading to take you into all those corners. I am not you though, so don't expect everything I share to resonate. I'm painting a picture to offer inspiration about the plethora of ways we can educate our kids and to share nuggets from the amazing places I've witnessed doing things differently.

This book is a translation and expansion of an academic thesis about self-directed education (SDE). SDE is a radical approach to learning which flips all that we take as truth about how humans develop on its head and allows the steering wheel to remain in the hands of the learner; challenging the very idea that the learning process requires external intervention.

Permitting a young person to take charge of their experiences and follow their instincts brings up all kinds of fear; hence we live within political systems and institutions where this isn't allowed. For me, this is because of our perceptions and assumptions about human nature. The self-directed 'schools' I visited during my research gave a glimpse as to what really happens when humans are allowed to lead themselves; a demonstration of what organic human nature looks like and how it functions when it is not forced from the outside. SDE is but one approach to learning and development and doesn't suit everyone. This is the biggest thing that I feel needs to shift.

By definition, 'one size fits all' is a myth; we all have individual needs and I want to see kids experiencing the approach that suits their individuality. In the coming pages I will introduce you to a few of the different approaches to education out there, alongside making my case for consciously giving kids more control over their lives and experiences. In recent years we've become so frightened of bad things happening that we've steadily reduced the freedom children have to explore the world and make their own decisions, correlating interestingly with a dramatic rise in mental health issues.

I want to make it clear that I truly appreciate the formal education I've received; the research and analysis skills I possess were developed through my experiences within academia. Through university my research mentality was formed. I learned to hold oppositional ideas and be able to explore them, extracting juice without surrendering to sit at the feet of the person who birthed the thoughts that inspired me. I learned to listen and explore without losing my sense of self. I found radical theorists whose words opened my perceptions and my heart. I would often find myself in the library quietly sobbing as I read words which embodied the struggle against oppression that is so deeply carried within humanity, feeling a fire in my belly that scorched my being into the desire to act.

That said, a powerful piece of research is often lost in the institution and rarely makes it out into the world to influence social change. And you're held by weird, old school, classist and patriarchal rules about how to speak and convey what you mean, without much space to put your feelings, passions and personal insights into the picture. I therefore decided, through a magical meeting with a very special Airbnb host (more on that later) to write a book in my own way, about all I saw and learned during my research adventures, getting it out into the world without clunky wording that makes your brain itch and your eyes want to bleed (perhaps that's just my experience of reading academic writings!). I hope to have achieved just that.

You'll notice that throughout the book I emphasise and de-emphasise things with grammar, inspired by the revolutionary bell hooks and her ability to highlight the way power relations are demonstrated through grammatical capitalisation. I also present The State and The Media as beings (nodding to director Wes Anderson and his character, 'Social Services', in the movie *Moonrise Kingdom* for that one). Writing a book instead of a thesis has allowed me to be playful and as you'll most probably discover, I like to play a lot.

Critical thinking for me is about deconstructing and adopting the seemingly childish notion of 'but why?' that sends so many parents bonkers. From sociology and history to politics, psychology and philosophy, the coming pages dig down to the roots of all things learning and education, exploring the thoughts of brilliant minds and the actions of phenomenal activists.

From the ideas that created and maintain the education system to the perceptions that we hold about children and childhood, into the origins of schooling and the various curriculums that are transmitted both atop and below the surface of the mainstream environment and the impact all of this has on the developing human, we're gonna deep dive into what is happening within classroom culture. I'll then introduce you to some of the alternative education philosophies I've studied and practices I've witnessed during my travelling research adventures, presenting you with the pieces I deem as important to consider when deciding what to do about school.

It is my intention to create sparks within the hearts and minds of people who read this book so that they can create change in the lives of the children closest to them. Micro-changes lead to macro-changes and revolutions always come from the bottom up. In my opinion, the next step in our collective evolutionary journey across the board, is about letting go of the notion that someone will create the changes we want to see on our behalf and instead utilising our communities and doing it ourselves. This is the whole philosophy of self-directed education - one leads oneself in collaboration with a community of others doing the same. The information and inspiration contained within this book is offered with the intention of empowering you to do just that.

Thousands of fascinating books, articles and theories have been playfully distilled into accessible language and coupled with stories of the remarkable people and projects I have witnessed putting it all into action, offering you a firm footing to step forward and to inspire co-ordinated, revolutionary action.

PART 1

(the stuff we take for granted about where we are)

WHAT *IS* CHILDHOOD?

The thing I love about sociology is that it takes us on a journey to uncover the roots that underpin what we see on the surface of life and society. It makes us ask questions that often we wouldn't even consider asking, highlighting just how daft some of our collective notions and ideas really are.

Structures and systems in society are built upon dominant ideas. We now know that a lot of the ideas of the past were absolute delusions, fuelled by violent dispositions that gave rise to terrible things. Although thought may have progressed from that point, the systems remain in place. To break a system is to unpick the ideas that underpin it, revealing absurdity and thus dissolving its power over us. When we understand (and see how ridiculous) the foundations of a system are, it no longer controls how we see the world and operate within it. Our actions and perceptions change, and it is from here that new systems can be built. Let's start with exploring what makes up our ideas and perspectives around children and childhood.

Generally speaking we view children as empty vessels, waiting to be filled with the wisdom of adults through family, schooling and experience. I'm not sure I can always see the wisdom that us adults have accumulated but hey, I'm part of the *snowflake* generation – we are way too sensitive and critical around the topics of social inequality and environmental destruction(!).

Defining childhood itself is quite a challenge, as it differs all over the world and throughout time. For that reason, people often describe it as a *social construction,* which basically means it is defined by the surrounding culture. For instance, when my grandad was a lad back in England in the 1930s, childhood was very different to what it is today. That said, throughout all cultures in all times, there seems to have been a distinction between children and adults. There is usually a period where children are given leeway as their ability to decipher right and wrong is developing as they grow (there's a rabbit hole there but we'll pass that one by for now). Childhood is generally perceived as a process of becoming an adult; a time of growth, development and immaturity before *real* life begins. And for reasons we will explore, the adult is much more valid within the eyes of our global society.

There are lots of different factors to consider when trying to determine when childhood actually ends. Children are growing rapidly throughout their first years of life and go through many different, fascinating phases. Post-puberty, however, the speed of development begins to settle down. Girls can become pregnant from their first bleed and so, from a biological perspective at least, puberty could be seen as the time that childhood is over.

Or maybe the completion of childhood is when young people are seen as adults in legislation, like when they are allowed to vote within their society, or buy alcohol, or have sex; but again, these milestones differ from culture to culture. We could look at the level of independence and responsibility young people are offered to define when childhood ends, but even within the same culture, socio-economic status (class) and gender have a huge influence.

Let's say we have two 13 year olds. One is raised on a council estate and cares for her younger siblings, helping her single mum out with childrearing and housework. The other is dropped at school every day by one of her married, working parents who provide for her every need and won't let her out of their sight alone (her twin brother is allowed to make his own way to school because he's a boy). Huge differences even within tiny pockets of society.

Childhood also looks very different across the world. I have spent a lot of time in India which saw my heart explode in so many ways! I remember one afternoon when my friends from Assam and I were climbing up a dusty hill to visit a monastery and I was being mocked (as per usual) for my dreadlocks. In all our pictures together, the guys are making little bird signs behind me as they said my hair was like a nest. Oh, how we laughed! Anyway, on this particular day as we climbed, I was utterly taken aback as I saw a group of kids between three and nine years old with pickaxes, smashing up rocks alongside their mum. Covered in dust and sweat in the baking midday sun, they put down their tools to shout, smile and wave as we passed. It was one of those moments in life where I couldn't comprehend what I was seeing. Child labour, right there in my face. And everyone, including the people I was trekking with, just accepted it as 'normal'. There were no distinctions between adults and children. It wasn't seen as right or wrong; to everyone else on that dusty hill, it was just a group of humans working.

I also learned that away from the tourist areas in India, there isn't much scope for begging and so, many of the uneducated turn to sex work. Sex work can be an empowering profession for many women in the west, but the people I'm referring to did not have a choice; it was a matter of survival.

One young woman, the daughter of a sex worker, explained to me that as a baby, she would be taken along to sit outside the hut whilst her mum visited clients. Once she was old enough (12 years old) she had to become a sex worker too. That young woman arguably became a fully-fledged adult at 12. It was a blessing to be meeting her in the grounds of an organisation called Snehalaya. Snehalaya provides a safe house for sex workers who want to leave the men in charge of them and find alternative ways of making money.

There is an innocence that children bring regardless of where in the world they are; a cheeky, playful, inquisitive energy, maybe because they haven't realised the weight of the world yet and exist in a space of discovery which lends itself more easily to wonder. I've met children that had loving and comfortable lives and others in really challenging situations, and though the spark appears to a greater or lesser extent, it is more visible with kids than with adults.

Regardless of when the period of childhood ends, the mainstream view is that children need to be moulded into worthwhile humans as their abilities and opinions are at best, undeveloped. As a collective, we believe that without intervention these wild little beings will not become successful adults. However, though children are vulnerable and need extra support, they are more able than we give them credit for, we just don't give them much opportunity to show us, often making all their decisions for them.

There are many people who have challenged the incapability narrative about children, some of whom you'll be introduced to later in the book, but for now let's have a little look at the ways that the freedom once afforded in childhood has altered and why.

Why Kids Can't Be Free

Something interesting has happened in recent years. Not long ago, it was normal for children to explore the world on their own terms. My generation in the UK would get kicked out of the house on a Saturday morning and wouldn't be expected back until food was on the table in the evening. In that space, we were independent of adults, trusted to be responsible for ourselves and developing all manner of capacities. From taking care of our needs, to working things out with others, to managing risk and tuning into our own hunger and thirst, we had the opportunity to explore ourselves and how we operated free from being watched, analysed and guided by grown-ups. We were developing our independence and self-reliance, really getting to grips with what it meant to be human and what it meant to be ourselves in relation to our peers. These days, in most developed countries, young people are lucky if they can play in the garden unsupervised without a neighbour raising accusing eyebrows at the notion of neglect.

An important thing to note here is class. I was recently part of a project which involved building a yurt and creating a compost toilet up on some land on the edge of a social housing estate in the north of England. I was amazed to witness that these kids were still being allowed a childhood. They turned up, found out what we were up to and spent the whole weekend with us, helping and hanging out. Their parents let them roam and trusted they would be okay. I'd guess that their homelives were probably quite challenging and their parents maybe weren't letting them roam free because they were children's rights activists, but it was fascinating to witness that old-school childhood still exists.

So why has childhood freedom changed for more 'privileged' families?

From where I'm sitting, I see increasing levels of anxiety due to all the ways we have been taught to fear the world. This fear has then become the driving force of 'responsible parenting'.

It's true that there are more dangers to navigate in the modern world. Cars are more and more prevalent. Parents don't want their kids roaming round the streets for fear of vehicles and so will often drop them off into the arms of other adults to keep them safe. It makes sense, cars can very easily kill children. But, in the same way that you or I have learned to take care when crossing the road, most children can successfully and safely move from one pavement to another without being hit by speeding vehicles.

The next little bit of the puzzle is our questionable friend, The Media. We began to hear more and more stories of terrifying things happening to children all over the world. The idea was planted that paedophiles were lurking in everyone's back garden and sadly, we took it as gospel. When we explore the statistics however, most child sexual abuse occurs within the family and if not, the perpetrator is usually a trusted family friend. News reports don't demonstrate a shift in the safety of the world, we just hear more these days about the awful things that happen. And when we do, it's sensationalised.

Did you know that The Media has no legislative (legal) obligation to tell the truth? There is nothing in place to 'fact check' the information that is pumped out and no punishment for lying. If they are discovered to be fibbing, a tokenistic couple of lines of apology might be shared… if we are lucky! It's usually too late by then, the hype has been created and often legislation which limits freedom has been introduced.

> *Right now, there is a whole, an entire generation that never knew anything that didn't come out of this tube. This tube is the Gospel. The ultimate revelation! This tube can make or break presidents, popes, prime ministers. This tube is the most awesome, goddamn propaganda force in the whole godless world. And woe is us if it ever falls into the hands of the wrong people...*
>
> *So, you listen to me. Listen to me! Television is not the truth. Television's a goddamned amusement park. Television is a circus, a carnival, a traveling troupe of acrobats, storytellers, dancers, singers, jugglers, sideshow freaks, lion tamers, and football players. We're in the boredom-killing business. So, if you want the Truth, go to God! Go to your gurus. Go to yourselves! Because that's the only place you're ever gonna find any real truth. But, man, you're never gonna get any truth from us. We'll tell you anything you wanna hear. We lie like hell...*
>
> *We deal in illusions, man. None of it is true! But you people sit there day after day, night after night, all ages, colours, creeds. We're all you know. You're beginning to believe the illusions we're spinning here. You're beginning to think that the tube is reality and that your own lives are unreal. You do whatever the tube tells you. You dress like the tube, you eat like the tube, you raise your children like the tube. You even think like the tube. This is mass madness. You maniacs. In God's name, you people are the real thing. We are the illusion. So turn off your television sets. Turn them off now. Turn them off right now. Turn them off and leave them off. Turn them off right in the middle of this sentence I am speaking to you now. Turn them off!*
>
> *'Network'* movie (1976)

The Media has also really distorted our perception of children. Let's for a moment view children as a *minority group* - a group of people outside of the dominant social group often experiencing disadvantage and discrimination as a result. I'm 'snowflaking' again but roll your eyes and then roll with me and see where we end up. The Media can label and describe this group of people in whatever way they choose. The 'hoody' culture was a biggie for this. Young people in the UK were openly called thugs and blanket-painted as dangerous, weapon-carrying thieves. How could you spot them? They'd have hooded jackets on.

Grannies were absolutely 'bricking themselves' (feeling super scared) at bus stops when young people at their side were simply keeping their heads dry from the rain. If the 'hoody' stories were about the LGBTQ+ or Black communities, they simply wouldn't be allowed. We wouldn't permit a whole social group to be judged en masse like that these days. There would be public outrage! But with children and young people, we lap it up! And they don't even have the footing to object. Adults rule the world; kids just have to get on with it.

Children and young people simply aren't welcome in most places, especially older ones. Nobody's mum wants 15 teenagers in their son's bedroom. "Sorry, you have to get out of the house if you want to hang out. But don't sit in the park intimidating the public. And don't sit in the bus stop to shelter from the rain either. There's no funding for the youth club anymore so that's off the table. Stay AWAY from empty buildings. Oh, and sorry no ball games allowed in these fields. You're also not allowed to skate here, and we've installed little bumps on the path to make sure you don't."

You're not welcome. You're not important. We don't appreciate you. We don't trust you. Your kind are too threatening. Is it any wonder teenagers have such a hard time and want to escape through social media or with a spliff and a bottle of cider? They are completely and utterly rejected from society.

In one breath, we are painting children as these vulnerable beings in need of bubble wrapping and in the next we are saying that they must be caged for the threat to society that they pose. Either way, keep them indoors and keep your eye on them!

This leads us quite nicely into another influence upon children's opportunity to be away from adults. The internet! We are all obsessed and will happily sit on our bums with eyes glued to a screen. And for parents, it's a free babysitter. Plug them in and you (finally) have chance to rest or do what you need to do. You don't have to worry about where they are or what they are up to. They are quiet, under your nose so nobody can judge or pull the neglect card and are happy as they're getting their screen fix. Even the most 'conscious' parents need a break. Computer technology is just there and it's absolutely fantastic! A whole world at the tip of our fingers. Building brains and gathering knowledge. Connecting and entertaining. But as with sugar, it's addictive. And though it has the potential to develop the mind, it can also be destructive. Overuse of computers creates more sedentary humans, who are detached from their bodies as well as the natural world.

That said, computers and phones do offer kids a certain level of freedom. The internet is a vast 'world' that they can navigate themselves. Even if sat in their parents' living room, kids get to be in control of what is happening as they surf the internet or chat with their mates, experiencing the autonomy that as we are exploring seems to be almost disappearing from childhood. Is it any wonder they love screens so much? Technology is the hub of our social lives now and young people are not separate from that. Kids want to be with their friends, away from adults, and if they can't go outside and experience that then creating social space through the internet is the next best thing. Social interaction, as we realised through the covid planetary story, is key for all of us.

So why don't we recognise kids' autonomy as being important?

To begin with, we live in a time of *neoliberalism,* which essentially teaches us that the purpose of life is about driving the economy (buying and selling) through competition. The key values are productivity and efficiency. For something or indeed someone to be valuable in modern society, it or they must be meaningful financially. What kids choose to do when they're not being forced or managed by grown-ups is rarely economically significant. We will explore this more deeply in due course but for now let's put that into context with childhood in general.

Children generally do not participate in buying and selling and therefore are at the bottom of the food chain. Their freedoms and rights are not really taken seriously because what they would like to do with their time is regarded as frivolous. We haven't protected children's right to get outside and explore on their own because we overlook the importance and significance of it. And let's be honest, the past 50 years have seen the world skyrocket in a way that we're still struggling to catch up to, never mind keep up with.

I found it fascinating to learn that when my parents were young, the dogs roamed around in packs, just like the kids. The desire to separate ourselves from our wild nature and domesticate into a more 'civilised' race has seen us suppress and control ourselves and each other in very interesting ways. We live in these tiny little boxes, isolated from the wider community, engulfed by depression and anxiety, consuming all manner of toxicity to cope. The kids, the dogs and the monkeys still roam round in packs in India and I tell you what, I saw more smiles over there than anywhere else I've been. Here in the west, however, everything and everyone is owned; all must be controlled and kept on a leash.

In 1989, the *United Nations Convention on the Rights of the Child (UNCRC)* was drafted. It's a document that outlines basic human rights with special regard for the different needs that children embody. Though most countries in the world have ratified the document (cough cough, United States, where you attttt?!), it doesn't have any legislative power. Countries can be frowned upon or experience a little finger wag if they aren't upholding the rights described, but that is as far as it goes. In the same way that so many civil rights issues are handled, the UNCRC appears to be more tokenistic than anything else. "Excellent, we have put children's rights on a piece of paper and people have promised to follow them... Now, moving swiftly on to trade deals..."

When we think of children's rights, it's often coming from a protective perspective. Create rules to keep children safe. But as we are discovering, the obsession with keeping kids safe is making the boundaries of the world that they can explore smaller and smaller. A large part of the UNCRC (which is an amazing document, I'm just grumpy because countries aren't held accountable when they don't uphold it) is about protecting children's **freedom** and their ability to take part in society. There are 40 rights outlined from basic things like food and shelter to non-discrimination and self-expression, civil rights and freedoms, protection from harm, family rights, health and welfare, education and recreation, and additional protections for more vulnerable groups.

All the rights are equally important but the aspect of the treaty that I would like to pull into focus here is Article 31.

1. Parties recognize the right of the child to rest and leisure, to engage in play and recreational activities appropriate to the age of the child and to participate freely in cultural life and the arts.

2. Parties shall respect and promote the right of the child to participate fully in cultural and artistic life and shall encourage the provision of appropriate and equal opportunities for cultural, artistic, recreational and leisure activity.

"Play. Really? Of all the things to highlight, you're gonna talk about play? Isn't this a book about education? And play is recreation, right?" I would love to jump in there with a big "WRONG!", but it is true that an element of play is about recreation. The invalidation of recreation thread could take us deep into the notion of the purpose of life and how capitalism and consumerism have slurred our perspectives about what we're doing on the organism we find ourselves floating through space upon, but perhaps that is for another book.

PLAY

Granting that childhood is playhood, how do we adults generally react to this fact? We ignore it. We forget all about it - because play, to us, is a waste of time. Hence, we erect a large city school with many rooms and expensive apparatus for teaching: but more often than not, all we offer to the play instinct is a small concrete space. One could, with some truth, claim that the evils of civilization are due to the fact that no child has ever had enough play... Parents who have forgotten the yearnings of their childhood - forgotten how to play and how to fantasise make poor parents. When a child has lost the ability to play, he is psychically dead and a danger to any child who comes into contact with him.

A. S. Neill

Before we break down the reasons play is a fundamental human right, let's have a look at how different schools of thought define it.

The first thing to highlight when we talk about play is that it has ALWAYS been here. The one thing shared by all cultures, in all times, is play in childhood. I personally find that fascinating. It is the most organic expression of human action and is perhaps *the* defining characteristic of childhood. It is ancient and primal and has supported us not only to survive but also to evolve. Humans do it, animals do it. It is fundamental to biological development and happens innately – we don't get taught HOW to play. It's not about the instructions and the Monopoly board (we enforce that later); it comes from somewhere deep within us.

When you watch little kids, you'll generally see the same kinds of play wherever you are in the world; building dens (shelters), hide and seek (running from dangerous animals), digging (pulling up food from the ground), building towers, water playing and dressing up. The theorist Bob Hughes talks about this as *recapitulation*, suggesting that when young humans are developing, they revisit evolutionary behaviours in their play to recapture and integrate the ancient awareness into their present consciousness. Pretty cool notion, hey? Play is so much deeper than we give it credit for!

If we again look at children as a social group, they have their own norms and practices that come from within their communities that adults don't tend to share. Play is children's culture and is what naturally occurs when they are not being instructed. In addition to the traditional play types mentioned, there are also trends that come at different times.

When I was at school, one craze was 'shag bands.' Little plastic bracelets that everyone collected and if someone snapped one of yours, the two of you had 'shagged' which as you will probably know from Austin Powers, is to have had sex! Sex at that time for the majority meant a cheeky kiss under the coats in the playground. Bless us. Though the bracelets were never marketed as 'shag bands', school playgrounds across the country were all referring to them as such! And this was before the days of the internet. Crazy! Play is mystical, and as I have already said, it *is* children's culture. In the same ways that we fiercely protect the cultural practices of other social groups, it is time for us to give an equal amount of weight and protection to play.

Mainstream schooling is warming to play and its importance. You'll notice that across the world, educators are promoting play as essential for learning, especially in the Early Years (before five years old). Play is now recognised as a fundamental aspect of learning and if a curriculum is in place for a nursery, it is based in play (well, an adult version of it, but a good starting point nonetheless!).

There is now extensive research demonstrating the ways in which play enables multi-sensory learning and development, supporting small humans to socially and emotionally advance, exploring the balance of co-operation and independence. The idea is that human growth, especially in younger children, is biologically programmed and accessed through play and exploration. I do find it odd that, as we grow, we imagine that the essentiality of play dissipates somehow, as if this drive just clocks off when we reach a certain age (I do find a lot of our collective thoughts pretty bizarre, though!).

My personal perspective of play is a bit more political. For me, play is what humans do when they are not being told what to do. Human rights are about protection AND freedom, and as I've already mentioned, with children we tend to focus on protection. I believe the 'why' underneath that is because we don't believe in their capabilities, yet we don't provide opportunities for those capacities to be developed because we don't believe in them. See the vicious circle?

The white man consciousness of western ideals that has spread across the planet is about agenda. There is always an agenda. I don't mean a group of rich men with cigars in a dark room kind of agenda - I mean a future oriented drive to what we are doing in the present.

Agenda distorts choice, and we indoctrinate our children into this warped perspective of life. Every choice must have purpose and the purpose is generally about 'making dollar dollar bill, yo' because, let's face it, we need to survive. There is very little space for doing things 'for the sake of it'. And that, I feel, is why we have such a thriving pharmaceutical industry, a prevalent drug and alcohol culture, a global mental health crisis, a weighty dependency on political systems that do not serve us… I could go on. The point I want to make is that our 'for the sake of it' moments are the nectar of life, yet they come at the bottom of our priority lists.

Going travelling can be a profound experience of play. Living in the moment, following your innate drive and instincts and allowing life to unfold instead of trying to harness it opens something inside. Humans' need to play; it is how we connect, it is how we process, it is how we come to life. When we forget how important this is and don't take the opportunities for free action that are available to us, we get ill and darkness falls within us. We go one of two ways then; push on as an overachiever and eventually burn out, or give up and drop into dissociation, adopting a lifepath that does not express our individuality or provide us with fulfilment. Either way, it ain't healthy! Play is fundamental to healthy, fulfilled adults and children alike.

My perspectives on play have been formulated through and are most aligned with *playwork*, the radical wing of the children's workforce that exists to protect and promote young people's agency and free action. At my core, I am and will always be a playworker. The official playwork definition of play (which comes with an irony as the whole premise of playwork is that play is not defined by adults) is that it is, *'freely chosen, personally directed and intrinsically motivated.'* This could be a slogan for life! How different the world would be if people felt free enough to choose, direct and navigate from within themselves!

The Awesomeness That is Playwork

Playwork as a field exists to advocate for children about the things that matter to them. The history of playwork goes back many a moon. In 1942, a guy called Carl Theodor Sorensen in Denmark watched children playing and noted their fascination and attraction to construction yards. In response, he designed the first ever 'junk playground' and the kids loved it! It inspired a very special woman called Lady Allen of Hurtwood, a British landscape architect, children's welfare advocate and influential figure within the children's rights movement, who vowed to create something similar in Britain.

London was a mess after the war and, as is usually the case, spaces for children were bottom of the priority list. Lady Allen made her case for the kids and though people supported her ideas, nobody wanted to live next to a playground. After much consideration, they found the perfect place, the bombsite! Utilising a space in the community that nobody had any interest in using, it provided the perfect mix of risky and thrilling opportunities to play, create and destroy, and didn't require the installation of any equipment.

On a deeper level, I marvel at this as a reflection of the transformation of pain. Scars from the terrors of war upon the landscape being transmuted into something beautiful and meaningful in new ways, by the innocence of children. Oh, I love this story so much! The word 'junk' freaked people out, though, and so they changed the name to 'adventure playground'. If you get ever chance to visit a proper one, you'll see pretty much the same things that existed in that original bomb site.

What we now think of as a playground is blasphemous to me as a playworker. A small, fenced square containing brightly coloured equipment and a bouncy tarmac floor, with strong rules forbidding certain behaviours and subliminal instructions dictating how to use each piece of equipment offers very little opportunity for play. These spaces are usually created by people that have no knowledge of or interest in play. They have to put a playground in the middle of the housing estate they are building so they jump on Google and get one ordered. Can you imagine how different the world would be if we consulted children about what they wanted? That's the world playworkers want to see!

Playwork isn't just about kids' playgrounds, it is about young people having a place in this crazy world which is their own. They get to call the shots. They get to control it. Together. As we've explored, back in the day when we used to be able to play out all day with our mates, we had the opportunity to take the reins of our reality a bit more. Children's opportunity to be in charge of themselves and their time is reducing at an alarming rate and the field of playwork exists to ensure that these opportunities don't disappear altogether. Playworkers create, maintain and fight for the things that matter to children, representing their needs and desires in the face of agendas that give very little consideration to what children want, if at all.

A special relationship is cultivated between playworkers and children which is based on mutual respect. Lady Allen clocked it back in the day - the adult is not there to instruct but to enable. "You want to build a thing? Okay... here's a hammer and nails."

"You have an idea you want to bring into fruition? Okay... let's make it happen." The playworker is there to serve, not to direct, and you have to consciously dismantle or hold back your conditioning to permit that. To only offer help when you're asked for it is a skill, as is recognising and processing the fears we often project upon kids.

Risk

Now, let's have a little look here at risk. We are all well scared of bad stuff happening. As kids, we often have much less fear and again, back in the day, we were able to have all the thrills of realising our capabilities as we climbed up those trees or did the naughty things out of eyeshot of our caregivers. But now that adults are watching all the time, those risks and indeed the learnings and development that comes through overcoming the fear and actualising the intention are almost impossible to be lived.

I remember at university, a lecturer was helping us to understand the difference between risk and danger, and how our fear distorts depending on the context. Climbing up a tall structure is risky. Giving kids planks of wood to build with that are covered in rusty nails is dangerous. See the difference? Not only that, when it comes to injury, there are certain scenarios where broken bones are totally expected, because we value the skills being developed.

A kid is gonna drop in on a halfpipe for the first time. They've got their skateboard poised and everyone around them is watching and cheering them on. We all accept that this could result in a broken arm, but we support it because skateboarding is a super cool skill that takes time to develop. Another kid is getting ready for a rugby match; they are probably gonna come out of the game with a black eye or a broken rib, but we value the game and understand that it is par for the course. See the weird contextual distortion? It is our responsibility as adults to check in before we spew our fears all over children. Effective risk management is crucial, but we have to operate this edge really consciously (and be mega thorough with risk assessments). When we give young people the opportunity to take and manage their own risks, they develop the ability to risk assess for themselves; skills we all need and require.

We have this thing in playwork called *benign neglect*, which sounds well edgy but is really about stepping back from the micromanagement role that has become the norm. As adults, we share the idea that to be in control of kids is to be responsible, but the reality is quite the opposite. When we don't give kids the space to work things out for themselves, they grow into dependent beings who can't manage their own lives. There's a bit of a phenomenon developing these days where 'kids' of 30 years old are still living at home and I feel this is linked to the rise of parental micromanagement and the dependency this develops.

The playwork approach is about holding back our expectations, too. One of my favourite humans is a professor called Fraser Brown. He's one of the original playworkers and has created incredible spaces for play across the world, working hard on the front line and changing the lives of many children (and students) with his huge heart, alongside being one of the top playwork theorists. He is a remarkable person. I remember in one of my personal tutorials, which were always such a blast, he shared with me a little story about the gut-wrenching experience of letting children lead the way. He was managing an adventure playground and the young people had built this huge, amazing structure together which took up most of the space. It was risky, fun and a marvellous creation. The kids had spent a lot of time and energy creating it and loved playing on it. He was super proud of them and what they'd made. One day, the children decided to have a bonfire - and up it went! They burned the whole thing to the ground. It is what they wanted to do. And so, they did. Poor Fraser.

This highlights the beauty of impermanence which is often really embodied on the adventure playground (the profundities of life are always revealed through children's play). Though the sites are fixed in location and open for a certain amount of time each day, the playgrounds are constantly in a state of change and transformation. It is a place free of agenda and is full of open-ended opportunities. One day there may be a draw bridge, the following day the same materials might be crafted into a swing, the following week the whole thing might go up in flames.

Playwork has a very empowering perspective of children, often lacking in educational, developmental and economic viewpoints. Alderson coined the term *being child;* a child valued for who they are and what they bring in the present. It's not about who they may grow into or what they represent for the future, nor is it about trying to mould them into something - it's about valuing them here and now. Playworkers see kids through this lens. "I see you as you are. I think you're really cool and valid as you are. Your needs and desires are just as important as everyone else's and I'm here to help you actualise them, as developmentally and politically you have additional barriers that I don't have."

Play to Heal

There are also many therapeutic benefits of allowing children to follow their innate play drive. Something powerful seems to happen when a person can process pain through play. At a conference, I met a man who had been a playworker his whole life in London. He shared with me a story that has stuck with me forever.

A teenage boy had come to the playground really upset and angry. He asked for a hammer and nails, which is very common in the playground. He didn't want to talk but the playworker could see he had stuff going on and so stayed close, but not close enough to interrupt what the young person was doing. After a while, he realised that the kid was making a weapon. Now, this is where the role of the playworker is an absolute art. Most adult workers would lose their shit and boot the young person out of the playground, throwing them onto the streets with all that pain. Instead, the playworker leaned in. He started asking the kid about what he was doing in a non-judgemental or authoritative tone. The playworker plugged into curiosity, even though he was understandably really scared. He knew he needed to continue to engage, meeting the kid in his pain and holding space for him. The pair ended up walking across the playground toward the fire (there's always a fire burning on adventure playgrounds), engaging and talking with weapon in hand. As the kid opened up, the playworker learned that something really tragic had gone down. The young person felt safe enough to share - in itself, a hugely successful intervention - but what happened next is the magic edge. Of his own accord, the kid put the weapon he had created in the fire and silently watched it burn. He was given space; he was trusted, he was held, and he processed. This for me is playwork.

A lot of playwork interventions happen in places of poverty with young people that have seen and experienced things most adults cannot even conceive of, where traumatic experience and disadvantage pours in through every aspect of their lives. Playworkers often become the safe adult for young people that don't have a safe adult in their lives. The adventure playground becomes the safe place for young people that don't have a safe place. And I know from my own experience, how crucially important these things are. A young lad in London from a low socio-economic background who seems a bit lairy can quite easily be written off and labelled before he's 13. His identity is set by those around him and becomes a self-fulfilling prophesy. Before you know it, he's in and out of prison and on a path from which there is no return.

When someone has a safe adult who can offer unconditional love, these patterns often break down as trauma can be processed instead of suppressed. In playwork, this love is called *unconditional positive regard,* a term borrowed and adapted from famous psychoanalyst, Carl Jung. "No matter what happened yesterday, even if you were all up in my face, I get that there's a reason and today is a new day. I respect you. We can try again. There are limits and you will be asked to leave if you can't uphold what we've collectively agreed in the space as 'rules' but I will never write you off. I'm on your side." Again, for me, this is the magic of playwork. And it gives you a ticket into childhood culture usually off limits to adults. Because you respect them, the kids respect you and let you into their world; you gain *honorary child status.*

The other beautiful thing that comes with these playgrounds popping up in disadvantaged areas is that they become a place for the whole community. Parents aren't usually allowed into the adventure playgrounds themselves but they will often develop relationships with the adults working there. As you can probably imagine, a playworker is a certain type of person and singing from a different hymn sheet to a social worker or a teacher. They don't hold the superiority card which comes with white collar professions, meaning they feel approachable and safe. It is a very different dynamic when someone wants to empower you instead of trying to save or fix you.

There are some awesome adventure playgrounds across the world but these days, the majority of playwork practice takes place in more mainstream settings. It can be a nightmare as, ironically, most children's services don't have children's desires at the centre. Playworker's advocate for children in these situations. The kids don't get invited to input, so a playworker is there to represent them, often up against people with very different agendas and ideas.

The essential component of the playwork definition of play is that it comes from within. If an adult has created an activity for children with a specific outcome in mind, it simply isn't play anymore. It has an external agenda; harnessing play to push young people into the adult form we have designed. On the surface, it's 'Oh look, we can make learning fun!', but I actually find it exploitative. A set of activities is not play. Sitting children down to do a colouring sheet or a game to learn about numbers is not play. Deciding on the goal and creating a path for the young person to follow to get to that outcome is not play. Though far removed from the way we all seem to operate, we don't need to manipulate kids to make them learn. I find it so fascinating that we have these intricate systems within our bodies, like the circulatory system, that enable the human being not only to function but to exist, and they are completely aside from the mind, yet we struggle to accept that the human mind is not the most powerful or intelligent force in our reality. Bless us.

To truly play with a child is to join their world. To let them call the shots and let them tell you what to do. In that realm, magical things happen. I once watched an amazing documentary which highlighted this wonderfully. I don't remember the name, but it explored the power of play to support young people with autism to develop relationships. The most powerful scene I witnessed involved a family that had spent years really struggling to connect with their son. He was in his own world and very unresponsive to them, which obviously was utterly heart-breaking. They were offered a tiny piece of advice by the professionals at the facility they were visiting, which was to **join** their son in his play. Mirror him. Do what he is doing. And lo and behold (I'm choking up as I write this), their son let them in. There they were, playing together. Their son spoke to them. They met. They connected. And all because they went to him, instead of trying to pull him into our weird world of overstimulation and form.

Roger Hart, a committed activist, influencer and theorist in the realm of children's rights, celebrates the way that playwork creates a truly *horizontal* working relationship between children and adults. The power distribution is equal. Humans meeting on a level. The playworker role is to facilitate the instinctual drive of the young person through creating the ideal environment. The adult is an almost invisible influence in the space. And I tell you what, it takes a heck of a lot of skill to become that. The playwork approach is a truly receptive, ear-to-the-ground way of relating to young people that also involves being hyper aware of the influence adults have over children, even simply by sharing space.

Children experience adults as authority figures in all areas of their lives. For some young people, this manifests as a desire to please grown-ups. When connecting with a child like this, they will be trying to entertain and prove their abilities all the time. They are not being their instinctual self; they are performing to receive love. For other young people, they want to push back and rebel against adults. When interacting with a child like this, they will often want to challenge boundaries and see how far they can go. Again, these young people are not embodying their instinctual self. Our adult influence is extremely powerful. Playworkers will often have their head in their notes or be 'doing something' simply to look busy. The trick is to consciously remove ourselves and our influence as much as is possible so that kids can do their thing. Play is so much deeper than it appears, as is the adult influence on children's behaviour, and playworkers really get that. Play is not only about development; it is the realm of free, unbridled and innate human action. And I would argue that this is the most important thing to be legislatively protected in the current times.

We've now established that play is learning, play is fun, play is development, play is a human right. But for some reason, we slowly wean children out of it, reducing opportunities for play as children progress through the schooling system.

THE FOOLIN' OF SCHOOLIN'

We don't often question the things that are the norm within our communities. School is definitely one of these facets. You go to school. It's important. And if you don't get the opportunity, you really miss out.

If you asked the average person what the purpose of formal education and schooling is, the response would be well-intentioned. Ideas around supporting young people to grow and develop and giving them the skills that they need for life would probably emerge. The general impression is about *banking* information into empty vessels. School is seen as an injection of knowledge, gifting hungry children the sustenance of education that at one time was only accessible for the privileged but which is now it is a right that all young people deserve and receive. The curriculum transmits a foundational understanding of a variety of subjects and creates a well-rounded being with numerous opportunities and the freedom to progress in society, following a path of their desire. Though the world doesn't necessarily reflect this truth, we drum it out again and again to young people.

I'm about to take us down a Matrix-style rabbit hole; the following information might just change how you see schooling forever more! Or it might lead you to conclude that I'm even more of a snowflake that you first imagined, but I urge you to read on.

A Little History

To start at the beginning, formal education as we know it has its roots in the Prussian schooling system. Frederick II, King of Prussia between 1740 and 1786, was a very progressive man, especially for his time. Though he rolled out a few oppressive orders, he reformed several systems during his reign that were mimicked throughout the world. During my research, I discovered that historians agree that he was an openly gay man, which makes him even more of a legend to me due to perceptions about homosexuality at the time. He became less of a revered character after the nazis glorified him, but I digress. The point I want to make is that Fred rolled out funded formal education to the masses and this was the first time we'd seen such a thing. Yes, he wanted to create a solid workforce. And you could perhaps see that through the lens of, 'he wanted to create a larger working class of slaves', but let's give credit where credit is due. At that point, schooling was the gatekeeper of information and knowledge, and until Fred broke the mould, it was reserved only for the privileged. The system he introduced gave the lower classes free education, trained teachers and provided them with a basic salary, funded the building of schools and established a formal teaching curriculum.

Around this time, the American Revolution was taking place. All the white, male, immigrant colonisers were fighting about who owned what and instead of American land being returned to its Indigenous community, the united states was established. This was happening almost alongside another kind of revolution – the Industrial Revolution. In britain, machines were on the rise and industry was being born. Both these events saw mass formal education become politically and economically important, and public/state schools (US/UK) were rapidly established in a similar fashion to the Prussian system (I could share more about the influence of the Rockefeller family upon this but I'll let you do your own research on that one).

This was the beginning of education as an institution where age groups and subjects were taught separately. Education spaces were no longer about hanging out, debating, exploring and cocreating knowledge in the ways of the toga wearing, ancient europeans. There was now a standard that every student must rise to and a binary curriculum with no space for questioning.

There are numerous facets that make up the mainstream schooling model. Most were birthed in Prussia and haven't really changed since. There is a foundational aspect to the approach which is that everyone learns in the same way. We tend to forget that child humans are just as diverse as adult humans and therefore the ways in which they interact with the world, take in information and process life is extremely varied. Some young people's needs align well with the following facets of our formal education model, while others, as we all know, do not.

This is How You Memorise

Though there has been little change in the mainstream schooling system, certain methodologies have been integrated in an attempt to meet individual needs. Though outdated now, the model of different *learning styles* is one of them. There were always the people at school that were better with books and the ones that were amazing at building and doing. This idea branched out into a theory around how to meet the needs of different kinds of learners.

You've got the visual learners that need to see things, images and such, to help them to retain information. Then there are the auditory gang that need to hear and chat about information they are trying to remember. There are the doers that need body moments integrated into their experience, and the readers and writers that need books and the opportunity to take notes. These pockets do tend to blur and are imposed over other elements, like whether a person is a solitary or social learner.

As I got older and went to university, I clocked that when self-motivated, everyone did their assignments differently. There were the night owls and early birds, people who really got into their flow at 2am, others that would dive into action after a solid sleep at 9am. There were those that took their time and others that would sit and attempt to do it all the night before, some that wanted study buddies and others that locked themselves away. I know this was influenced by other things like how much people partied, but there are folk that really thrive busting things out last minute. With all this considered, how can a teacher possibly meet the needs of 30 kids in a classroom?

Another part to bring into focus here is about learning. Are we suggesting learning is remembering? Or are we aiming for understanding here? I need to take notes to formulate understanding, but when I learned to spell my birth name, it took marching around the kitchen and putting the letters into song.

There is also variety in the approach to teaching in schools. We have the most common and most traditional, which is *teacher-centred*. The adult at the front of the classroom holds the power, transmitting the necessary information from a textbook to the class, expecting/praying that they retain this information to pass the upcoming examinations. It is down to students to take in what is being shared, silently writing on a very tidy page in black or blue ink. Clean, quiet and conventional. To encourage this process, there is a strong reward and punishment scheme. If the child does not meet the expectations projected upon them, they will be coerced with threat of punishment or temptation of reward. Get your gold stars, be a good girl/boy or get a telling off and be banished from the room, group and experience.

Student-centred teaching methods are a little more popular these days. The curriculum is more spacious and kids can influence what they are learning. Though there is an expected destination in terms of level of understanding and an ability to demonstrate learning, how the students get there is really down to them. Learning happens through independent and collaborative exploration where the teacher is more of a facilitator. Assignments are often co-created between teachers and students, giving kids more responsibility and greater space for creativity. There is also often a technological component so they can conduct their own research instead of relying on a textbook with limited parameters. We'll see an inspirational example of a student-centred setting a little later in the book, but it's important to note that this approach is almost impossible to match up with traditional examinations in mainstream schools. When there are specific learning outcomes and bodies of text to be memorised and understood for an exam, there must be a strong funnel to direct the young people to the information necessary for them to ace their test.

The bold and radical teachers I've spoken to that manage to integrate adventure, play and excitement into their approach have often come up against strong resistance from other staff. Finding ways to make the school experience fun is a big task, but then having to deal with your colleagues being upset as the kids become 'disruptive' due to the excitement cultivated in your classroom must be soul destroying. One person shared with me that you have to choose whether you do right by the kids or right by the system (sigh).

Seriously Important Subjects (100 Years Ago)

The late and wonderful Sir Ken Robinson was an educator and all-round inspiration who dedicated his life to drumming up the necessary impetus to revolutionise the education system. He was the first person to wake me up to the reality of schools. I mean, I always got it on a deeper level. Questioning authority is part of the fabric of my being. But the way in which Ken brought light to certain aspects of mainstream schooling really hit me; he delivered a strong call to action that my cells immediately responded to. He openly, humorously and intelligently criticised the curriculum within our present standardised education system, and all of sudden, I just got it. It was the first day of my undergrad journey with university and my body went into chills as I witnessed him. That moment genuinely changed my life. It was where my passion for education reform began. *'Do School's Kill Creativity?',* is one of the most viewed TED Talk's ever. If you haven't seen it yet, stop reading and watch it.

When schooling was first created, the curriculum was a match. As we've already covered, universal education in the 1800s was about equipping the working class with the basics of what the workforce required at the time. Obedience, efficiency and productivity were skills key to industry and therefore important and relevant jobs were waiting for young people on the other side of their schooling journey. Information was not accessible in the ways it is now. Unless you were born into wealth, there wasn't space to stop and educate yourself. There was no welfare state; you had to take what was on offer for work or you would literally die. The higher classes were always well-educated and the moment that schools began to open to the poor, it probably felt like a potential remedy to class inequality. The working class were being offered entrance to a place that provided a ticket to the world, where children could become literate and rise above their predecessors' stations through developing skills and knowledge. Physical subjects were less valid and creativity even less than that because, at the time, these things did not meet the needs of the economics of society.

My grandparents were raised in extreme poverty and there was a lot of emphasis on educational success when I was growing up. Though she had paid work at certain times, from 19 years old, my grandmother raised the children and ran the household. She cooked three meals a day for herself and my grandad (along with anyone visiting) until he passed when she was 88. For my grandpa, becoming educated was the way of proving one's worth within society. Though he left school at 14, he rebelled against his mother who wanted him to work forever in the mill (and pay her accordingly), forging his own path and furthering his education at night school. His experiences in childhood taught him that if you are poor and uneducated, you will be ridiculed and rejected. This fuelled him to create different things for himself and to ensure the rest of the family did the same. You can imagine that my nomadic, free-spirited, usually broke, dreadlocked and unconventional ass was a pretty challenging taste to swallow and by heck did we clash sometimes, just like he did with my mom in her youth. At other times though, we could really go down the rabbit hole, sharing our intergenerational perspectives and musing upon life together, memories I will forever cherish. He was a great man.

Anyway, I think we can all agree that the world today is calling for very different things than in the previous century. To begin with, the technological revolution has changed everything. Can't spell? Can't do basic math? Not a problem, the device you carry in your pocket will do it for you. At one time, knowledge was only accessible through institutions whereas now, in the information age, content is free and co-created. Wikipedia is a fantastic example of this. Anyone can alter and update entries. This does mean that its reliability is seriously questionable, but even that is of benefit, as it encourages us to think critically. Discernment is a key skill for the world of now. We live in a moment of unbridled access to information that we can access anywhere in the world. Anything we don't already know, we can look up on the internet in an instant and, as we will discover in due course, research suggests that when we are stimulated by desire as opposed to obligation, we are much more likely to retain what we have discovered.

Throughout the world, we are also currently witnessing the importance of critically examining what we have been taught and why we have been taught it. What is knowledge? How is it constructed? Whose ideas and research conclusions are we sharing, and why did they make the cut over others? All information outlets have an agenda, whether they are broadcast through trusted television networks, written in academic journals or shared on video blogs. Find the agenda and you'll usually be well on your way to uncovering the level of trust you should be offering to the reliability of such information. The opportunity to question the underpinnings of delivered information doesn't appear to have reached school classrooms, though. The subject matter is delivered as 'fact' but is often a distorted perspective that has been influenced by power relations.

For example, with history as a subject, whose history is actually being shared? I distinctly remember being taught about 'european explorers that "discovered" the Americas', reinforced by images on colonial tea towels and china cups at my grandparents' house. When we take a closer look at what happened at this point in history, however, we see that europeans went all over the world massacring Indigenous communities and stealing their land. In order to fit the colonial agenda, when the stories were shared, the Native people were de-humanised and framed as 'savages' who didn't even have the footing to claim the land that their people had lived on for generations, due to their less-than-human status. His-Story is written to celebrate and validate the perspectives and actions of the oppressor.

The accounts of information we are presented with are opinions. Always. And as I've already mentioned (but wish to really drive home), these opinions create narratives that society then functions around. The irony is that the further up the educational ladder we go, the more we are encouraged to think critically. When we reach university level, we are forced to question everything. The purpose of education at this stage is to unpick and to unravel. A 180-degree turn. If you question the curriculum between the ages of 5-18 years old, you're called out for being disruptive and often punished (speaking from experience here) but if you do the same as an under/postgraduate student, you'll land yourself top marks. Say whaaat?!?

I believe there is great potential to create change within society through the introduction of new paradigms of thought into mainstream schools, even as they function at present. To create space to critically examine the curriculum would be very powerful. Grading kids in relation to original thought instead of how well they can memorise and regurgitate would be a game changer. But an approach such as this would go against the *hidden curriculum* being transmitted within schools.

The Curriculum Behind the Curtain

School is the advertising agency which makes you believe that you need the society as it is.

Ivan Illich

Ivan Illich is another fascinating human who has been very influential upon my perspectives. He was a homosexual man, a philosopher and a Roman Catholic priest - how's that for some world bridging? Perhaps because he functioned outside of the expected norm, he was also a progressive social critic. His book *'Deschooling Society'* (1971) is one of my favourites and is definitely worth a read. In fact, that book unexpectedly reappearing in my life, led to this book being written. Within it, Ivan deconstructs the purpose of schooling, proposing that the state agenda is often very different to the mainstream narrative. He coined the term *hidden curriculum* to describe what is being taught under the surface at school.

These subtle imprints are transmitted in different ways; the most obvious is through the physical environment. The structure of mainstream classrooms upon conception reflected the workplace of the time, the factory. Specific seats and assigned tasks, timetabled with a bell, was replicated in the environment that the majority of students would end up in, creating a disciplined, punctual workforce. Why do mainstream classrooms still mirror a factory floor? That's not the world that awaits students on the other side of their education. And what do we learn from this set up?

There are many pieces of the *hidden curriculum*; subservience to an authority figure, the normalisation of hierarchy, the requirement of self-abandonment and an emphasis on grades over learning or enjoyment, all preparation for successful life, right? The message is to submit, obey and please, and you'll get on just fine. If you don't do that, though, you're going to face hefty consequences. Schooling teaches us again and again, that authority is external. And though this can be related to policing, let's just stick with the idea for now that authority is about choice.

Throughout childhood and especially in school, the locus of power is taken from inside and placed in the hands of another. We continually reassert that this is what human beings need to grow into themselves and function in society, often overlooking that our societies do not appear to be running in alignment with health, for humans or any other living being on the planet. There is also a hierarchy to external authority. Someone above is always presenting the person or people below with what they need to do and what they need to know. The teacher receives the curriculum and is trained in the pedagogy by the governing body of the system. This same notion applies whether the school transmits a national or an alternative curriculum. Though the content may be very different, the approach is the same, replicating the hierarchy reflected throughout society. 'They' present the 'what' and we do it or learn it.

The most overwhelming reality of school is CONTROL. School controls the way you spend your time (what is life made of if not time?), how you behave, what you read, and to a large extent, what you think. In school you can't control your own life...

All the time you are in school, you learn through experience how to live in a dictatorship. In school you shut your notebook when the bell rings. You do not speak unless granted permission. You are guilty until proven innocent, and who will prove you innocent? You are told what to do, think, and say for six hours each day. If your teacher says sit up and pay attention, you had better stiffen your spine and try to get Bobby or Sally or the idea of Spring or the play you're writing off your mind. The most constant and thorough thing students in school experience - and learn - is the antithesis of democracy.

Grace Llewellyn

As Grace so powerfully highlights in her book '*The Teenage Liberation Handbook*' (1991), when looking at the schooling model through a political lens, we see a dictatorship. There are a set of rules that the people (the students in this case) have no influence over. There is no alternative media; the syllabus is taught through official textbooks. Thought and speech are suppressed; you can only speak in the classroom with permission and you must echo back the 'correct' information. The people in power, teachers, have not been elected by the people, the students. How are we meant to function within a supposed democracy when all we have experienced is a dictatorship? Unless we actively study politics, the curriculum rarely teaches us anything about democracy and what it means to be a citizen of such a thing. Pretty bonkers really when we break it apart.

Paulo Freire, another remarkable human, in his book '*Pedagogy of the Oppressed*' (1968), suggests that we exist within a social order that to a greater or lesser extent gives us all an experience of oppression. He says we then subconsciously find ways to become the oppressor within the dynamics available in our lives, to elevate ourselves and mask the feelings of persecution we are personally experiencing. The book explores these ideas in relation to the dynamic between teachers and students.

Schooling makes a lot of sense through the perspective of an innately flawed general public, lacking the necessary characteristics to function well. To build the ideal human character, we must be restricted, shoved into uniforms and sat at desks, having to ask permission to speak, to pee and to drink. The idea that we all subscribe to, whether knowingly or not, is that there are certain qualities that we all must strive toward and the only way to develop those qualities is through following the path that 'they' preach. But who is the mysterious 'they'? And do they really know what's best?

You (Don't) Got the Power!

Though it is invisible and happens almost by accident, schooling consistently disarms our ability to exercise and hone our innate power. It sets the trend and lines us up for life with an overarching system of governance, teaching us that someone else has the reins and whether or not they are trustworthy and have our best interests at heart, we must submit to them. If we don't, we will be punished/lose the job/ruin the relationship. In one way or another, we will have a huge price to pay. Dodgy actions of authority figures are either justified because they are 'allowed' by the overarching rulership or their responsibility is negated because they 'had to do it' to follow appropriate protocol. They usually cannot be questioned and the rules that they have created without consultation must be upheld, it's just the way it is. If we do not submit, no matter what the injustice, we will be detained and have our freedom taken away. The power is hierarchical and the person with the most authority has the final say.

The whole notion of governance comes from the mentality that someone else is more equipped to do it for us. It is the idea that our internal natural authority is not enough somehow and that normal humans are innately incapable of living in community. These are the narratives that our society has been built around. We can look at race, class, gender, age, physical ability, all social groups are generally subservient to another group that are more powerful because they are allegedly more equipped and therefore superior, deserving to rule over.

This pattern is EVERYWHERE: teenage bedrooms, offices, management boards, local communities, countries. And we justify it over and over again, alleging that people cannot be trusted to make their own decisions. I feel it's riskier to trust people in positions of influence, you've got to have a will of steel to not get drunk upon power.

I used to think that *anarchy* was about burning down the system and getting a mohawk but the more I've studied the theory of anarchy, along with deconditioning my mind and reclaiming my personal power, for me, anarchy is about liberation. And ironically, it comes with a heap of trust in human nature. Another one of my favourite humans is Colin Ward, a theorist whose gentle spirit truly separates the notion that you have to be an aggressive punk to be an anarchist. He extensively studied the ways in which society functions and took particular interest in children's play to prove his findings. Read his work. It's fascinating.

In his book, *'Anarchy in Action'* (1973), Colin suggests that anarchy is operating underneath the surface of our societies all the time. Yes, we have the rules on the surface, but underneath that are always small-scale community networks that function somewhat outside of those rules. This was demonstrated beautifully in my local area when we were in lockdown and the state failed to meet the needs of the people. Local businesses offered free food to those in need, neighbours became allies taking care of one another and we, the people, teamed up. We self-organised in a very anarchistic way and Colin would argue that this is a reflection of true human nature.

I don't believe that anyone can teach us without also learning from us. We are here to share our learning. You and I, together. Sometimes I'll be listening to you, then you'll be listening to me, and our ideas will cross-pollinate, forcing one another to question, forcing one another to grow. I actively reject the idea that we are less or more worthy than anyone else. And from what I can witness, the humans that have any form of societal or philosophical wisdom have cultivated it through expelling the internalised bullshit that the surrounding society has injected them with. They said no, they went inside, they found answers and they lived radically against the imposed order of the time. It could be argued that this a little more difficult in the 21st century as the space from schooling to workplace is much more reduced and the numbing faculties we have developed, from screen entertainment to substance abuse (whether sugar or heroin) has filled a lot of the space that would have previously presented us with the opportunity to reflect and find our inner teacher.

Prove Yourself

Another piece of the education picture is about performance. We live within a target-driven culture. Everything is about demonstrating our progression in alignment with the ideals that surround us. And progression is demonstrated by results. Doesn't matter what we are doing to the environment. Doesn't matter that people are burning out at 30 years old. The only thing that matters is to push and meet the target, it is the key to the system. It brings money. It brings status. And we are set up for this trend through our experiences with examinations in school.

Success within standardised testing is sold to us as essential for opening the necessary doors to a stable life. The way in which we measure intelligence at school (which is apparently the most important quality of the human being, develop that head!) is the same as it has always been: through rote. A successful student can memorise facts, theories and processes and demonstrate these memories in an exam where they are unable to discuss with peers or rely on literature (books or now the internet). This made sense at the time of the Industrial Revolution. Memorisation of facts was applicable to many jobs. But is memorisation a key skill for success in the 21st century? Memory processes that we have regarded as the intelligent capacities of cognitive function can and will be beaten every time you put a machine next to a human.

Examinations are created by The State and educators in schools have no influence over them. No matter how much a teacher opposes the curriculum or testing, their hands are tied. Their job is to ensure students pass exams, enabling them to access college or university. This is often an argument that keeps parents from plunging into more radical expressions of education. I mean, who wants to limit their kids' future by not providing them access to the qualifications, sold as essential for success? Yes, their kids may be struggling and having an incredibly difficult experience in school in order to get those qualifications, but if they don't have that opportunity, surely it is neglectful parenting?

I am and always have been rubbish with exams. Short-term memorisation and fact recall just isn't my thing. If a theory interests me, I will retain it and be able to weave it in with all the other theories held in my noggin, presenting some pretty cool arguments and ideas when I'm writing or chatting to folk. I'm a geek! Full on. But I don't remember facts and specifics. I'm a nightmare with people's names and you should never let me drive without a sat nav!

I remember so clearly at 11 years old beginning to be prepared for the formal examinations that would take place when I was 16. I flunked most of them. It really affected my self-worth and the choices available for the next step of my education journey, but I needed to have that experience as it led me to unpick the system and the fabric of life itself. I became a free human. Had I 'succeeded' at that point, I would have probably got stuck on a hamster wheel feeling lost and empty. And I did get to university, three times.

Who's the Best?

Let's not forget competition. At school you are constantly encouraged to be in competition with those around you. There is an average and you are either above or below it. You must aim to be the best and if the person next to you does better than you, that should stimulate you to do better. Schools also compete through league tables where exam results are published and compared. Parents choose where kids go based on these results and governments often offer financial rewards to those higher on league tables. It's such a mess!

An interesting piece to explore here is the way in which this competition structure morphs within culture. Pierre Bourdieu talks about something called *cultural capital* - I learned about this through Miss Dynamite's little brother, Akala, in his book '*Natives: Race and Class in the Ruin of an Empire*' (2018), another corker of a book to read. Anyway, *cultural capital* is essentially what is valuable within a culture. If you fulfil the criteria, you have the ticket to acceptance and progression within a community. Each group has its own specification for what gathers the most respect.

You've got a bunch of lads not really bothered about their grades but they love to push boundaries and humiliate teachers. Being loud and disruptive and 'not giving a f**k' is what will bring you the most respect; it's the *cultural capital* of the group and each person competes to see who can be the loudest badass. You've got the girls that have (heartbreakingly) subscribed to patriarchal notions that correlate worthiness with sexual attraction and 'prettiness' - the shorter your skirt and the sexier you rank with the boys dictates your ranking within your social group. This could be perceived as evidence that competition is an innate characteristic of human behaviour, but if we hadn't been through the education system, would it be present? My research with young people that haven't been exposed to the intense conditioning of traditional schooling suggests otherwise.

Competition may stimulate some people to grow, but I question the cost. There seems to be a transmission of corrupted ideas at every level. If you are one of the 'gifted' kids, you are often under loads of pressure to maintain your perfect grades (and behaviour). If your marks sit in the middle of the group, you receive the message that 'you're average' and don't have anything special to offer. And if you're at the bottom of the class, you learn that you're a failure within the collective. Though I don't believe that competition is necessarily toxic, the ways in which it integrates with the development of self-worth as kids are growing can affect them for life.

Where the Life Skills at?

Though we live within a culture driven by performance, the modern workplace (as is demonstrated by organisational management development) values *soft skills* related to communication, collaboration and the development of ideas. At present, these are biproducts of the social aspect of schooling and are nowhere to be seen in formal examinations. Ironically, fact recall and binary thinking is seemingly the opposite of what workplaces are looking for. Innovation and relational skills are now much more valuable than an ability to retain vast amounts of information.

Even for management positions, leadership is becoming less about domination and hierarchy and more about creating an environment which inspires and enables people to contribute their gifts and talents. Projects are usually collaborative and rely upon up-to-date research from the internet or literature, as opposed to facts from school that swiftly become outdated. Even if school exams are passed with flying colours, this no longer guarantees you a place in the workforce. Graduate employment is plummeting and the majority do not take a position in the field they studied.

Mainstream school offers very little in terms of life skill development. Teachings about money management, health and wellbeing, an understanding of politics and all things relationship are occasionally squeezed in by revolutionary teachers, but the syllabus is so fixed and so full that essential understandings for adult life must be learned outside of school (around crazy amounts of homework!).

The Free Babysitter

Schooling has always been the largest and most fundamental facility for the economy. As we know, back in the day, this was because the economy depended upon people with a standardised cognitive skillset to match the industrial demands of the time. Now, however, schooling is essential for the economy because it provides childcare.

Before I deliver this point, I want to claim that I am a proud Feminist. The world would not have progressed this far without the Women's Liberation Movement and my life would be not a speck of what it is without the brave women that came before me. I am eternally grateful and dedicate my life and work to the lives that were and continue to be lost in the struggle for women's rights. Reclaiming the female, both through individual lives and the feminine qualities we have collectively damned or disregarded, will save the world. Feminism has and continues to transform our collective for the better and has given women like me opportunities that simply would not have been available in previous generations. Freedom fighters are my people. Radical social action makes my heart swell and eyes leak with fierce passion and inspiration. But the opportunity for women to enter the workforce has really altered the landscape of childhood.

Children are now placed in the hands of The State much earlier than in the past; the same State that is arguably rooted in oppression. From two years old, the most formative time upon consciousness and human development, children are separated from the people they have (hopefully) developed a healthy attachment to and are put in the hands of strangers. Strangers that often embody very different qualities and priorities to those that have been present in the home space. We need to put the kids somewhere to make the money we need to survive and preschools/schools are where they go.

If we are honest about it, the most important consideration is convenience, distance to home, opening hours, places available.

We have a look round and make sure it feels safe, sussing out the adults and how the kids are, but that's about as far as it goes if our child doesn't have specialist needs. We don't tend to have space to consider the depth of what it means to send our kids away; everyone does it and our priority has to be getting back to work.

Having children is a biological urge that I am now really experiencing hormonally, but the reality of parenting is different to how it has historically been. As was really highlighted recently with the implications of the global pandemic, when the workplaces and schools closed, modern parents and children were together more than they ever have been. In some ways, in a more natural set up. And everyone lost their s**t! We aren't really used to what it means to be around small humans all the time and we've lost the community piece essential to childrearing. Establishments and institutions have swooped into remedy this (arguably after creating the community breakdown in the first place) but we are therefore conditioning children into the norms of a less than harmonious society earlier than ever before.

TRY Harder

There is another illusion that we use to justify schooling. *Meritocracy* was another gem from Akala's book. It is the idea that hard work will get you anywhere. Put children in school so they have the opportunity to work hard and achieve their dreams. The *meritocracy* message is reinforced consistently throughout schooling and society, nothing is off limits if you put in loads of effort and develop the necessary skill. The thing is though, this logic does not take into account what has to be in place for a person to put in said effort.

Psychologists have noted the influence of childhood trauma upon healthy development and have created an official list of *Adverse Childhood Experiences* (*ACEs*) for young people to be assessed through. Essentially this is about creating space for greater compassion. If a professional understands that a child is traumatised, they are less likely (hopefully) to react aggressively toward behaviours that are deemed inappropriate to display and to provide a greater level of intervention to support the young person. ACEs range from divorce to bereavement, neglect, parental mental illness, incarceration, substance abuse and domestic violence, attempting to encompass all forms of disadvantage that can happen before a young person reaches 18 years old.

When people have experienced multiple *ACEs*, they face invisible barriers to success that the notion of *meritocracy* does not consider. You see, *meritocracy* works for the privileged. I feel it is important to note here that privilege is not just about the economic status of a family, it is about all aspects of life: relationships, health, opportunity and wealth. Someone can be mega rich and incredibly neglected, while another can be poor but surrounded by love and stability. I saw a wonderful video of an American teacher with his students in a line about to take a race. He read out the *ACEs* one by one and if a student had not experienced that particular trauma, they were invited to take a step forward. By the end of the video, you had young people staggered across a field, some almost at the finishing line before the race had even begun demonstrating that effort is not the largest component in 'success' within the schooling system or the creation of a seemingly functional adult life. Sometimes a kid that has been through a lot will sail through life. Often, though, the trauma that results from *ACEs* is a barrier to everything, and neither reward nor punishment are remedies.

The scientific field of *epigenetics* is now exploring intergenerational trauma. The research is mind-blowing. *Epigenetics* reveals that the imprint of trauma is carried within DNA. Not only is it carried but it also has the power to affect the behaviour of genes, and thus the behaviour of the organism/the behaviour of the person. Our genes are affected by our ancestors' experiences. Even young people with a low *ACE* score can exhibit unhealthy behaviour due to a genetic imprint of their parents and grandparents' adverse experiences. Trauma and responses to trauma are inherited. I highlight this to question why schooling, considering it allegedly exists to grow healthy humans, has no therapeutic intervention built into it when most people, young and old, are seriously traumatised. Like, c'moooooon!! And just as an 'eh' sidenote, I am unaware of any country which has a psychological screening process for teachers (or politicians), which feels irresponsible to say the least.

Big Business

At the time of writing, a new UK law is being proposed in relation to education. It is argued to be about raising standards and ensuring all children access high-quality provision, but many people are concerned and questioning its motives. The 'Schools Bill' will give The State greater authority to monitor and assess home educating families, posing quite a challenge for those who do not believe in outcomes and following the national curriculum (more on that piece later). Amongst lots of other things that will reduce freedom and flexibility within the landscape of education, the paper also states that all schools will transition into 'academies.'

Most secondary state schools in the UK (for young people aged 11+ years) are already academies. Schooling has become privatised, and it's happened under the noses of the general public. Academies are independent of the local authority and are registered as businesses. They are legally and financially autonomous, receiving government funding to distribute as is deemed fit by an internally selected board of trustees, with no independent body to oversee responsible action being taken. There have been lots of controversial events around academies. The majority of 'leaders' or headteachers employed within academies are managers with no experience of teaching or working within education settings. Many academies are owned by trusts that run a cluster of schools receiving funding for the cluster, with absolute freedom of budget. The Academies Enterprise Trust came under fire for paying headteachers in excess of what is possible in the local authority and employing independent contractors that were either the board members themselves or close relations, exploiting the schools and the children for personal gain.

The argument for academies is that they are a godsend for failing schools. Successful business owners rush in to rescue and bring grades back up through strong management models. Many academies have failed, jeopardising the educational experience of the young people. Teachers in academies have reported a lengthening of working hours, a dramatic reduction in pastoral support for kids and stricter rules which do not consider the children themselves.

I find anything that isn't transparent suspicious and like I mentioned, the privatisation of education has happened in a pretty sneaky way. The general population hasn't been aware that schools have been steadily shifting into academies. The recent Schools Bill made it appear that they are 'proposing' the idea but most schools have already been privatised. I'll let you muse upon that one.

Now we've pulled mainstream education apart a little, I'm gonna introduce you to some of the more radical approaches to learning and school, but first, it's time to get far, far-out. Imagine we're having the following conversation sat on the floor at 3am with pizza, herbal tea and anything else you might want to add into the equation...

WORMHOLES AND THE QUANTUM WORLD

Often the argument is that schooling prepares children for the world they have been born into. An initiation into life. But in the same way that the syllabus doesn't really line up with the modern technological reality we find ourselves part of, what we are teaching isn't in alignment with what we now know of how our world and reality functions.

Full disclosure. This is a bit of a bonus chapter. I really wanted to write about wormholes and the quantum realm and I've woven it in tediously before introducing you to Rudolf Steiner, the first of the alternative educators we will be meeting. He was all into spirituality and science. I accept that this might not really be in alignment with the topic of the book and shared more because I'm a ridiculously far-out person. Reality is well weird, though, and I like peeling off the wallpaper we've plastered on the walls of our lives to try and normalise things. I'm not sure if you played 90s platform video games but when you finished a level, there would often be a 60-second bonus round where you jumped all over the screen collecting extra coins, apples or eggs. So here you are, my loves. Extra eggs for you all.

The 'laws of nature' that ground-breaking scientists have discovered - like gravity for instance - are seemingly straight forward on the surface. And again, they become the notions that our reality functions around. Here's where it all gets a bit funny. We all know Einstein's name but have we as a collective really digested what he was on about? As I started digging into these topics, I discovered that perhaps we are still all operating through a more Newtonian perspective of the world. Isaac Newton was the dude who had an apple fall on his head and realised that gravity was a thing. But Einstein was like, "Wait a second, that is true, but there is much more going on here."

Albert Einstein was alive between 1879 and 1955. I personally found that really surprising. As an early 90s child, it absolutely twisted my melon that Einstein was on the planet the year my dad was born. Albert came from a Jewish family and they moved around a lot, eventually leaving Germany and living in Italy. He didn't get on well at school and openly criticised the methods used (reciting facts), but this kid was a genius. By the time he was 13, he'd overtaken his tutors, driven by the notion that all life could be understood through maths and was diving into philosophy through Kant, a scientist who was led to philosophy through his research. Despite his genius, when he was 16, Einstein failed his school exams! He excelled in maths and science but failed the general test.

A few years passed and he renounced his German citizenship to avoid military service, missed the boat with his sweetheart and ended up at college where he met Mileva Maric. She was a pretty remarkable woman and the only female on the course. The pair fell deeply in love. It makes me buzz to imagine them curled up in bed getting far-out and debating together or just eating toast with a cup of coffee. Later, they had a son together, Hans, who sadly had a breakdown and was diagnosed with schizophrenia when he was 20. By this point, Albert and his wife had separated, but Mileva cared for her son throughout his life, whilst he was in and out of hospital. After she died, Hans went into hospital permanently.

I like to tell these little stories about Big Names to humanise them. When we imagine these thinkers, we often know little about them and it's easy to forget that they were people, just like us.

Imagining Albert all loved up or grappling with the reality of having a hospitalised son makes him more relatable to me. And if I'm going to listen to someone's ideas, I want to know who they were/are.

Einstein was far-out. Like proper far-out. And he found the evidence to prove his far-out notions. His theory of relativity revealed that space and time impact one another more than we thought. The speed of time changes depending on where we are located!

> *The theory of relativity was revolutionary because it showed how the speed at which time happens is mutable; that space and time are not discrete entities. Time and space and motion (i.e. movement through space) collapse into a fourth dimension, in which all act on each other. It is impossible to say "now" without saying "here" and "how fast".*
>
> *Aida Edemariam*

We've all been leaving Einstein's theories at the door as we haven't managed to wrap our heads around it; thereby, we are seeing things through a really clear-cut and also rather mechanical understanding of how our reality/world operates. We aren't perceiving the whole truth. Our understanding of the wider universe (and beyond) and our place within in has expanded a lot even since Einstein was around. I find it really surprising that we collectively seem to dissociate from the fact that we are a spinning ball of matter floating through space. People always look at me weirdly when I bring this up. But it's absolutely mind-bending! The way that we function despite knowing that we are spinning ridiculously fast and don't feel a thing, for me, is phenomenal to sit with, and proof that human perception is limited.

The sky totally blows my mind too. What we see as blue sky in the day is an illusionary reflection of the sea bounced back from the atmosphere, the little bubble which surrounds the Earth as we meander through the galaxy. There is no such thing as mundane through my eyeballs. We, as humans, are not able (as yet) to hold these notions and discoveries and function with that awareness switched on. Would your life look different if you really integrated the understanding that our perceptions are illusions?

In the centre of our Milky Way galaxy is a black hole. Black holes are dead stars which create a vortex of energy, pulling the surrounding matter into their core, due to the collapse of gravity that happened when they died. The *Einstein-Rosen Bridge* theory suggests that because time and space warp in black holes, they could likely connect different locations and times. Say what?! Potentially, at the centre of the galaxy that our solar system is rotating around is a *wormhole,* a bridge to different locations in the multiverse, in a physical place and time sense.

Though Einstein was one of the first to hold this theory, he proposed alongside it that it would be impossible to journey through it due to *spaghettification*. Yes, THAT'S ACTUALLY A SCIENTIFIC WORD! The portal would be so unstable (due to the gravitational collapse) that anything passing through it would become a string of atoms. I used to have a playdough tool when I was a kid that this reminds me of: you put the dough in one end, popped some pressure on a little lever and hey presto, you got spaghetti on the other side.

In 1963, Roy Kerr jumped in and was like, "Wait! If everything in the universe is rotating, then the hole will be doing the same thing, too. If you avoid the middle (*singularity*), you should be able to ride that portal and pop out the other side." The probability is that the hole would collapse whilst the journey is being taken, but there is a potential. And I like potentials.

> Now assume that a pair of twins, named Maggie and Emily, are standing at either end of the wormhole. Maggie is next to the wormhole on Earth in 2009, while Emily is on the spaceship (also, for the moment, in 2009). She goes on a little jaunt for a few days, traveling at nearly the speed of light, but when she comes back, thousands of years have passed on Earth due to time dilation (she is now in 5909).
>
> On Maggie's side of the wormhole (still 2009), only a few days have passed. In fact, the twins have regularly been discussing the strange sights that Emily has witnessed over the few days of her journey. Emily (in 5909) is able to go through the wormhole to Maggie's location (in 2009) and, voilà, she has travelled back in time thousands of years!
>
> In fact, now that Emily's gone to the trouble of setting up the portal, Maggie (or anyone else) could just as easily travel from 2009 to 5909 (or vice versa) just by stepping through it.
>
> Andrew Zimmerman Jones

FAR OUT! Maybe this explains the spaceman glyphs that appear all over the ancient world... Maybe our future selves popped back for a hello?

Also very interesting is that when we zoom in, in, in to a solid object, the majority of what we see is actually space. Tiny bits of matter, held together somehow through the nothingness which surrounds it (*dark matter*). And it's all vibrating. For example, a chair seems like a solid object. I can sit on it. I can throw it around. It's a real thing. But when we take a closer look, really what is there is emptiness with a little bit of matter. It's mainly nothingness. Which is boggling. And here we reach the gates of *quantum physics.*

A lot of the spiritual gang that want a bit of footing for their seemingly wacky notions about the ways in which reality operates (often discovered through meditation, lucid dreaming, during a near-death experience or when using psychedelic drugs), go absolutely off the wall for the tiny aspect of quantum physics they understand. Or maybe that's just me. But regardless, the quantum world is phenomenal. Experiments have revealed that these tiny (quantum) particles behave differently (the laws which govern them change) in reaction to being perceived by human consciousness (somebody's mind). When viewed at a subatomic level, light shifts between appearing as particles and waves. It literally changes. Can you imagine if you were sat in front of someone and they flickered in and out of solidity? THAT IS WHAT IS HAPPENING IN THE QUANTUM WORLD. When we look deeply, the laws we believe reality functions around disappear, and it's because we are watching. We affect it. <u>We affect matter</u>. Quantum physics is such a trip! For the people in the know with 20 PhD's, and also to you and me.

I love science.

There's this strange illness throughout humanity which sees us as separate from one another, from the planet and from reality on a much larger scale. But quantum physics reveals that life is completely interlinked and ridiculously personal; each of us, simply existing with an ability to perceive, is astronomically powerful. Reality is held by mysterious forces that we are interacting with, whether we are doing it on purpose or not. What if we stopped pretending that life is dull, heavy and mechanical? There are so many things about the ways in which the world functions that we cannot comprehend, and to stop ourselves from freaking out, we've turned our awareness off. But what if we channelled the feelings that we can't rationalise into wonder? Instead of, 'woah, that feels scary and the ground doesn't feel solid, where do I hide?', how about, 'wow, this is totally magical and mind-blowing, I love this experience!'.

I feel like children start in the magical mind-blowing space but then we condition them into a more 'serious' and rational, mechanical perspective of life. Mainstream schooling and the human sphere of living we have created around it moulds our mind to think and perceive the world in a very specific way. Once the mind is conditioned, we continue to see through that lens (unless we dismantle the conditioning). And it limits us. It limits our capacity for awe and connection. It limits our ability to love. Can you imagine what would happen if school existed to facilitate the opening of children's minds instead of moulding them? And if these deeper mind-boggling truths were considered when constructing a curriculum?

PART 2

(alternative approaches to education)

RUDOLF STEINER

Many alternatives to mainstream schooling exist and I'm going to introduce you to some of the more well-known set ups. We'll start with the most far-out system that is surprisingly one of the most popular. Its curriculum was actually created with an awareness of the mindboggling aspects of our reality.

Steiner/Waldorf schools exist all over the world. I've had the pleasure of visiting and working within some and wow, they feel so good - gentle and considered. Though popular, it's rare to find people that know much about the roots of Steiner education, so hold onto your knickers, we're going in!

Rudolf Steiner was part of a late 1800s/early 1900s movement of thought which I would say pioneered the exploration of analytical science through spiritual experience, or perhaps they explored spirituality from an analytical perspective. Regardless, these guys claimed to be very psychic, balancing channelled insight with ancient Eastern thought and scientific theory/enquiry (I was born in the wrong era...). *Channelling* is based on the notion that we are one big soup and everything that has ever happened or been conceived by us as a collective can be accessed by an individual human mind. And I mean, if wormholes theoretically exist and our little minds affect the behaviour of matter, why not! The idea of our interconnectedness is often compared to the individual cells that make the whole of 'you'. All the cells that make up your body are connected to your consciousness. The cells are individual but you are a whole being and operate as such. A lot of the New Age ideas adopt the theory of the universe as one big brain that can be plugged into, uploaded to and downloaded from, like the internet. We can access information in altered states, like in meditation, trances or when using psychedelic drugs.

The thing I most buzz off about this gang is that they were well far-out, deep thinking and super spiritual, but they were also fully committed to social change. Like a group of stoners that DID something with their insights and inspirations. They didn't hang out at the weekend and then return to conditioned living; they crafted new systems and dedicated their lives to creating change for the collective. Steiner schools are a living representation of this legacy.

The group was established by 19 people in New York City in 1875 but after a few years, they anchored their headquarters in Chennai, India. They called themselves the Theosophical Society. Breaking away from the Roman Christianity that had become the predominant western path of spirituality, their philosophy was about personal relationship with the Divine through the cultivation of spiritual wisdom; *theos* meaning God/Divine and *sophia* meaning wisdom. Their tagline was *'an unsectarian body of seekers after Truth, who endeavour to promote Brotherhood and strive to serve humanity.'*

The Theosophical Society was the forerunner to the Hermetic Temple of the Golden Dawn established in 1887, a magical secret society of prominent esoteric thinkers, teachers and initiates such as Dion Fortune and the infamous Aleister Crowley. Unbeknown to the majority, these are the roots of the New Age philosophy which exploded in the 1960s and 70s and which continues to blossom throughout non-religious spiritualists the world over.

Helena Petrova Blavatsky (1831-1891) was a key player within the Theosophical Society. Though she was a very controversial person and has been repeatedly 'damned', she's another of my favourite humans. Her life was devoted to spirituality and travelling across continents to explore the depths of our reality, to do this as a lone woman in the late 1800s was unheard of. Though clunky and written in archaic language, her work from 1888 (what a cosmic numbered year), 'The Secret Doctrine', is a collection of profound and powerful writings about the spiritual nature of reality, the principles of which formed the foundations of the Theosophical Society. Though she wasn't always in the seat of power within the group, her visionary capabilities and learnings from the East (I mean, this woman was a travelling spiritual seeker before it was even a thing) continually guided the movement. Not long after writing 'The Secret Doctrine', her earthly life ended and Rudolf Steiner joined the gang.

Though lots of people in the modern New Age movement feel that psychic kids are a new thing, they have been referenced for a long time. Steiner was apparently one. He claimed that he was always open to the non-physical realms and by 15 years old had grasped a spiritual understanding of the mechanics of time. He was a gifted writer and incessant searcher, so the Theosophical Society was a perfect fit. By 1902, he had risen to become the general secretary of the German/Austrian branch of the movement.

Blavatsky brought forward the notion of ascended masters and spiritual entities that oversee the evolution of mankind. Within theosophy (again echoed in the New Age movement), 'Christ' meant the innate divinity within every single human, whether embodied or not. Before her death, Blavatsky prophesised that at the end of the 20th century, a new teacher would come to the Earth to lead a united humanity, when the divisions and biases have almost been eradicated and literature is easily accessible to the masses (oh, hello internet). This new leader would be the next

Christ being after Jesus, someone with their divine spark embodied and popping off. A real-life ascended master. Her Theosophical Society successors, Besant and Leadbeater, took the message following her death but shifted the timeline and claimed to have found the prophesised being in 1909. They ran with it; and this was arguably the beginning of the end for the Theosophical Society.

Jiddu Krishnamurti (1895-1986) was a child from a small town in India who didn't get on well at school but was seemingly very sensitive and somewhat psychic. His mother, who he adored, died when he was 10 and his father, a theosophist since before Jiddu was born, retired from his career and uprooted his family to take a job as a clerk for the Theosophical Society. It was then, when Jiddu was 14, that the society discovered him. Besant and Leadbeater decided that he was the chosen one, the one who would lead mankind to enlightenment. Along with his family, he was swiftly moved to live within the headquarters of the Theosophical Society and his life radically shifted. He began being raised in preparation for the influential life he was apparently destined to have.

Steiner and the German/Austrian branch of the Theosophical Society had already begun to disconnect from the global movement and Krishnamurti's entrance into the gang tipped him/them over the edge. Steiner couldn't and wouldn't accept the claim that this boy was the saviour, and he broke away from theosophy, birthing his own ideology: *Anthroposophy* (*anthropo* human and *sophia* wisdom). One of the main reasons Steiner could not accept Krishnamurti as the next embodiment of Christ was because of race.

> *One can only understand history and all of social life, including today's social life, if one pays attention to people's racial characteristics. And one can only understand all that is spiritual in the correct sense if one first examines how this spiritual element operates within people precisely through the colour of their skin.*
> Rudolf Steiner (Vom Leben des Menschen und der Erde)

Steiner claimed that in non-whites, the spirit, 'takes a demonic character and does not completely permeate the flesh; there, white skin does not appear. Atavistic forces are present which do not let the spirit come into complete harmony with the flesh.' (*The Christ-Impulse as Bearer of the Union of the Spiritual and the Bodily*).

There is a lot to be said for Steiner's philosophy when it comes to social reformation, children and education, but what the f**k?

My first steps into alternative education were within a Steiner school. I began the training course to be a teacher and worked in a beautiful little school. But when I posed the question of Steiner's racism to modern anthroposophists, whether teachers or simply initiates, the response is always along the lines of, "C'mon, it was a sign of the times." No. I won't accept that. He came from a movement, the Theosophical Society, who embodied a very different stance.

The three objectives of the Theosophical Society are/were:

1. To form a nucleus of the universal brotherhood of humanity without distinction of race, creed, sex, caste, or colour.
2. To encourage the study of comparative religion, philosophy, and science.
3. To investigate the unexplained laws of nature and the powers latent in man.

Top of the list: all humans are equal. They literally make reference to race. Yes, the larger global picture of the moment was influenced by the f**kery of colonialism. The portuguese, spanish, british, german and other european countries were de-humanising Native people as they competed for world domination, giving rise to the horrendous slavery trade that ensued where human beings - children, women and men - were traded as goods. They had to disconnect from the atrocities they were committing by reducing these fellow humans to 'savages'. My heart bleeds for what has happened. I have cried so many times into books as I learned real history. But theosophists didn't embody these corrupted beliefs. It is not an excuse for Steiner. Stop letting him off the hook.

A little while ago, I saw a quote from someone in response to people deciding to no longer listen to a prominent world music group as their lead singer was being questioned about paedophilia and sexual assault. The music from this band inspired the hearts and minds of hundreds of thousands of people on the spiritual path. As the lengthy Facebook comment battle grew, this one dude swung in and said something along the lines of, "If a tree has a rotten trunk, take it's fruit but don't sit under it." This idea has stuck with me and been applicable in many different situations, and I want to put it on the table now. I won't sit at Steiner's feet. I won't glorify him. But I will examine and receive the inspiration and knowledge he embodied utilising my own discernment. And I invite you to do the same. See the whole picture. Look at all sides. And then take what works and aligns with you.

It's important to share here that Steiner schools were not supported by the nazis, and during the regime, they were all closed down. Steiner's ideology, however, seems to align with the notion of white supremacy, and this is one of the things I can't get over. Most modern anthroposophist's feel he maybe got it wrong about race whilst demanding that his approach and philosophy are followed to the letter in Waldorf education settings. This makes no sense to me. If his ideas can be questioned in certain contexts, surely it is okay to review and adapt Waldorf education to align better with modern life?

One thing that I really rate about Steiner was that he put energy and focus into social reform. He recognised that spiritual enquiry required another step: systematic change. He was a spiritual activist. It wasn't just about gathering with like-minded people to develop and explore consciousness through ritual and philosophical enquiry; it was about translating all of that and using it to inform new ways of being. Not just 'getting off' on spiritual experiences or liberating oneself, he instead wanted to bring the learning from those experiences into the core of the systems that humanity functions around. Creating spaces for people to be in tune with the spiritual reality as we do our human thing. He also birthed new methods for working with the earth; agriculture in harmony with the seasons and moon cycles - *biodynamic farming* – which, again, is really far-out but brings some very interesting results.

Steiner is a household name (for people that know how to pronounce 'quinoa') because of the schools he created. And this, for me, is the part that I respect him for. He *did* create change. He was an activist through creation and innovation. And his legacy lives on.

Steiner/Waldorf Schools

Someone you rarely hear about in the field of Steiner schooling is Emil Molt (1876-1936). The first Steiner school was actually his idea! Emil was the director of the Waldorf Astoria cigarette company (which still exists and owns some very swanky hotels across the world). He was a theosophist that followed Steiner into anthroposophy. Molt had already been offering free education to the employees of his factory in Stuttgart, Germany but realised he really wanted to offer education to children. It was 1919 when he approached Steiner with the invitation to create the pedagogy for a school for children of workers of his factory. Steiner took the reins, visioning and creating the teacher training and syllabus, funded by Emil through the cigarette company until the teachers requested that the school became private. Though few people know about Emil, the schools are known interchangeably as Steiner/Waldorf schools due to the name of the cigarette company. Big ups to the invisible people of history who don't make the cut to become immortalised.

Steiner recognised the fatal flaw in the education system (which hasn't changed much since his time) as the development of intellectual faculties above all else. The core of his alternative approach was a curriculum to educate the 'heart, hands and head'. The method aims to gently ignite the internal capacities of the human and work in harmony with the soul, creating space for both creativity and intellect.

When you walk into any Steiner school, there is a certain look and feel. I remember my interview really well; I'd never been in such a warm and gentle environment with kids. Such a stark contrast to mainstream school. Smiling, happy children, passionate teachers and a building which hummed with positivity. Pastel-coloured walls and beautiful artwork on the chalk board created lovingly by the teacher. It smelled and felt safe. Though Steiner built his education system upon some very unconventional ideas about how human beings develop, you don't really see that in the classroom. Parents usually have no idea about the 'why' behind the things happening at certain times or in peculiar ways, but they still trust it as the children seem to blossom in lovely ways.

Formal 'instruction' doesn't start in Steiner schools until seven years old and though progressive political systems (like in Norway) adopt the same notion, it's for very different reasons. Modern day decisions to hold back on formal schooling are generally rooted in the recognition of the magic of play; Steiner's ideas were a little different. Our Rudolf was all about reincarnation and soul contracts. Steiner claimed to have channelled the truth about how a human comes from beyond the veil and into the human experience and this, my loves, is what his whole educational philosophy is based upon.

The journey to land fully as a soul into a human body, he said, took 26 years! And he believed that teeth were an indication of the incarnation process. Yep, that is not a misprint - teeth were super important to him. I must admit, I do find it curious that we have one set of teeth that fall out before our 'proper teeth' grow, and then we have the teeth that come through ages after the rest of us has finished growing. It's a bit weird, isn't it?

Steiner believed that the first birth was the one that we all usually consider as birth, when one pops out of mama's vagina. He said it with a little more tact, however, highlighting the importance and impact of entering the world as a separate entity through detaching from the physical mother. Though we have all been through this process, it is quite the initiation! I personally find it fascinating that spirituality often leads us back to this notion of oneness, as in reality it is where we all came from. We literally grew from another being and then popped out into separation, often with surgical scissors and very little warning. What a (traumatic) trip!

Anyway, the first *birth* in Steiner's eyes was from mother into the world and our first teeth embody the energy of our physical and family lineage, separate from our individual soul. Our own vibe hasn't even landed yet. Our human selves are simply a reflection of our mama. During those first few years, our ancestral selves are being moulded by what we see and experience. Alongside being completely dependent, we are gathering data about what life is all about.

According to Steiner, at this point in our lives, we are mostly existing in the spiritual world but have one eye open in the material world. He really emphasised that we shouldn't condition children out of the realms of imagination until the proper time because the soul is still hanging out beyond the veil. To train children to 'think' and see life through adult eyes when they are little is to rob them of the awesome experience of being able to bridge the two realities. In Steiner Kindergartens, which children can attend before they are seven, everything is formless - even the dolls have no faces! The method in his madness is that the more blank and gentle the slate in those early years, the better. Everything is about rhythm and song and softness, discovering the world through play and allowing the being to exist in both the spiritual and material worlds.

The second *birth* from his perspective was when the baby teeth fall out, around seven years old. This is where he believed we needed to begin formal instruction. All aboard the conditioning train! Though I take everything in life with a pinch of salt, after working with children for a long while, there is something interesting that seems to happen developmentally at seven years old. It always makes me smile. These kids with gangly legs and half their teeth missing, exploring their will and starting to shine their individual personalities out into the world, somewhere in between little and big.

I won't go into all the different birth points, but Steiner believed that as children progress through his system, they are presented with the curriculum that matches their spiritual and physical developmental stage. It feels important to also share that Steiner only trained a handful of teachers, delivering one, two-week course with three 'teachings' per day. What he shared in the lectures was written down and is the totality of the completely fixed system of schooling that Steiner presented, though the training has now been extended into a course usually taught over two years through weekend immersions, weaving in other aspects of his esoteric thoughts.

There are some truly beautiful aspects of Steiner schools, which is what attracted me to them to begin with. For starters, the students and adults are on first name basis, there are no uniforms and inside you find grown-up humans that are dedicated to young ones. Steiner teachers don't end up there because they have a degree and can't get a job in their subject area like many staff in mainstream schools; it's a calling. Though I don't mean that in the sense of spiritual destiny, Rudolf Steiner really did. And throughout the teacher training, there is a strong emphasis on self-reflection, steering people away from projection. In the morning before the kids arrive, the class teachers gather to discuss things but also to meditate. If there is a child struggling, they will be brought to the attention of the group and each day the teachers send them love and pray for them. How gorgeous is that?

Steiner's far-out notions and spiritual beliefs aren't taught directly to the kids, it's more that these ideas underpin the approach. There are rhymes and songs which relay some of his philosophy to the children, though, which I struggled with. Anthroposophy has strong gnostic Christian roots - an interesting blend of Christian notions and New-Age philosophy.

Each morning in class, the kids sing or recite poems about spiritual reality through an anthroposophical lens and the Christian festivals are celebrated with rituals. If we facilitate experiences for children to access their own connection with the deeper aspects of our reality, without overlaying our thoughts, beliefs and impressions, I can slightly get on board. But teaching children the idea's that we've taken in as truth and decided are universal truth feels icky for me. The songs and rhymes, no matter how much they may align with certain notions I've adopted about the nature of reality, felt to me to be programming children, which feels a bit culty.

One of the Christmas ceremonies I experienced was beautiful. A spiralling path was created with candles, almost like a labyrinth, and the children walked one by one with an unlit candle to the centre, lighting it from the flame of the burning candle in the middle before circling back out with their flame alight. I LOVE THAT! For me it symbolised journeying into the core of who we are to find our light and return from the underworld alive and kicking. But allowing the individual person to create the context and understanding of the experience in any way they choose is the important bit for me. In some ways, Steiner seemed to really embody that idea, too. Each age group studies certain myths and stories to explore the archetypal nature and initiations of being a human. The stories are told, the characters and themes are explored and what the young person draws from them is personal.

Creativity in Steiner settings is a funny one. On one hand, children are encouraged to decorate their pages, so looking through one of their workbooks will be a bright and colourful experience. They are given the space to interpret their learning in ways that feel good for them, drawing their own understandings and thinking creatively, illustrating as well as writing about their learning. But when it comes to more directly creative subjects, they are taught to replicate. They recreate paintings that already exist. They recreate sculptures that already exist. You'll see a wall filled with variations of the same picture, created with the exact same materials. Steiner apparently has his reasons as to why this is what needs to happen, but I'm not sold.

I broke the mould when I was there and faced quite a lot of criticism for it. My mascot for working with kids is a teddy called Eric. Flat Eric (yes, the guy from Mr Oizo's song *'Flat Beat'*). Kids love him, and so do I. He's been with me to many schools and helped facilitate some really cool workshops, including an awesome six-week mindfulness project called, 'I am amazing and I love myself!'

As part of my work with Class 3, the kids decided they wanted to create a theatre piece that we would perform for parents. I supported them to write the story themselves and as Eric was such a big part of our lives, he featured strongly. It was silly. It was funny. It was creative. Bananas were heavily involved. And everyone created puppets. They looked weird and wonderful and messy. And they were created by the kids, in their own ways, for their own reasons. In my playworker eyes, the performance was an absolute success! But for some parents and teachers that were used to performances that recreated something that the kids had been taught, it didn't go down too well.

When compared to mainstream schooling, Steiner's process gives much more space for children to embody themselves and develop gently; smaller class sizes, genuinely invested teachers, sweeter environments, a positive intention for the conditioning experience, creative encouragement, imagination, embodied learning, interacting with and teaching all aspects of each being in the classroom, games and play, and an intention to better the human race - it's definitely a large step in the right direction. But the curriculum hasn't been updated since it was created and is vigorously protected. The modern world has shifted a lot and there is, therefore, a growing disconnect. I would love to see the curriculum and approach updated to align better with the world we now live in. And I feel that the reason so many parents see their kids growing gently within the Steiner system is less about his methodology and more about the removal of the toxic aspects of mainstream education we've already explored.

KRISHNAMURTI

Remember the reason Steiner turned his back on the theosophists? Jiddu Krishnamurti? Well, though that kiddo didn't turn out to be the next messiah, he grew into a pretty remarkable person that created some waves of his own.

After his discovery by Besant and Leadbeater in his early teens, Jiddu was raised to be a global spiritual leader. After some controversy, both he and his brother ended up in the custody of Annie Besant and the Theosophical Society. In 1911, the Order of the Star from the East was created to prepare for Jiddu's influence upon the world and in the years that followed, whether because of innate skills or ones developed through the practices he was taught, Krishnamurti grew into a powerful speaker and writer that would often wow audiences across the world with his insights. Most theosophists were sold that he was indeed the proclaimed messiah but the more Jiddu grew, the more that he began to question it.

In 1922 after settling in Ojai, California, Jiddu had a life changing mystical experience which he referred to as *the process*. Just a few years later his brother and best friend, Nitya, died. It seems as though this was Jiddu's tower moment; the difficult and traumatic events in life that suddenly change everything, usually leading us (after lots of pain and sorrow) to a better place than we were previously. In 1929 he gave a spine-tingling speech to around 3000 of his followers refuting claims that he was the messiah and stepping down from his position.

I maintain that truth is a pathless land, and you cannot approach it by any path whatsoever, by any religion, by any sect. That is my point of view, and I adhere to that absolutely and unconditionally. Truth, being limitless, unconditioned, unapproachable by any path whatsoever, cannot be organized; nor should any organization be formed to lead or coerce people along a particular path... This is no magnificent deed, because I do not want followers, and I mean this. The moment you follow someone you cease to follow Truth. I am not concerned whether you pay attention to what I say or not. I want to do a certain thing in the world and I am going to do it with unwavering concentration. I am concerning myself with only one essential thing: to set man free. I desire to free him from all cages, from all fears, and not to found religions, new sects, nor to establish new theories and new philosophies.

Jiddu Krishnamurti, aged 30 - 3rd August 1929

(SATURN RETURN VIBES)

He denounced their labels, broke free of the cage they had placed him in and vowed to do his part to set man free, believing that is only possible through self-reflection and self-direction.

In a way, all that he went through with forced learning and being 'chosen' meant that he lived through and awoke from the illusion that he was somehow special and more able to access and embody divinity than others. He saw the idea of 'chosen ones' reflected in different ways across society and made it his life's work to break down this notion. Jiddu was highly against guruship and fiercely opposed indoctrination. He travelled all over the planet helping people to heal the urge to sit at another's feet and supporting them to find their own path of truth. He shared insights to heal separation, empowering people to develop deeper relationships with one another, the natural world and themselves. His mission, until his death at 90 years old, was to wake people up to their conditioning and foster greater embodiment of peace and love.

Jiddu had some very cool friends including Aldous Huxley; the infamous philosopher and author of *'A Brave New World'* (1932) and *'Doors of Perception'* (1954). His other bestie was David Bohm, often referred to as one of the most influential theoretical physicists of the 20th century. Y'see, Krishnamurti was all about collaboration between fields to explore truth from different angles. He was fascinated with reality and eager to heal the separation between different ideologies whether religious, political, philosophical or scientific.

Krishnamurti Schools

Jiddu was always passionate about education and started speaking on the topic when he was just 17 years old. Throughout his life, he founded several schools.

The foundations of his education system are:

1. Global outlook: A vision of the whole as distinct from the part; there should never be a sectarian outlook, but always a holistic outlook free from all prejudice.

2. Concern for man and the environment: Humanity is part of nature, and if nature is not cared for, it will boomerang on man. Only the right education and deep affection between people everywhere will resolve many problems including the environmental challenges.

3. <u>Religious spirit, which includes the scientific temper</u>: The religious mind is alone, not lonely. It is in communion with people and nature.

Krishnamurti schools are set in beautiful locations, surrounded by nature with well-equipped libraries and laboratories, inviting classrooms and well-qualified staff. They follow a rather mainstream curriculum but the big difference is that self-reflection is viewed to be just as important as gathering knowledge. Equal weight is given to the syllabus and the cultivation of the inner relationship which then extends to relating with others.

There is less distinction between teachers and students and a recognition that all are developing and learning in the space. The children are not in competition with one another, they are actively encouraged to work together and share their understandings, learning in mixed-age groups without a reward and punishment scheme. Kids are taught how to grow their own food, often being involved with the cooking of meals at school and working alongside teachers to clean and maintain the space.

Loving, mutually respectful relationships between staff and students are seen as crucial to the approach and the young people create their own individual learning path, with the help and support of tutors.

Oak Grove in Ojai, California runs from pre-school through to 12th grade and *Brockwood Park* is a Krishnamurti boarding school for 14-19 year olds in Hampshire (UK). The rest of the schools exist in India. I met a couple that used to work at Oak Grove, they shared that though the philosophy felt very in tune with child-centric and decentralised learning, in practice it felt quite similar to mainstream education with conscious 'add-ons'.

I can't say too much else about the schools as I've not visited one, but I wanted to share as our Jiddu had already been mentioned and I like him. It's interesting that though he and Steiner shared theosophical roots, the way they approached education was very different indeed. Somehow Krishnamurti's experiences seemed to ground him and direct him toward the idea that everyone has an individual path to truth, whereas Steiner believed he had found the formula toward enlightenment and conditioned kids in alignment with that notion.

There are lots of videos on t'internet of Jiddu sharing his vibes and I really enjoyed his books too. He embodied an anti-authoritarian energy and was a deep philosophical thinker (my kinda guy!). Oh, what I'd give to go back in time and attend a dinner party with Krishnamurti, Huxley and Bohm!

MONTESSORI SCHOOLS

Another well-known alternative education system is Montessori. Maria Montessori was born in 1870 into a relatively wealthy family in Italy. Her dad was involved in a tobacco company (like Emil Molt) and her mum was an educated woman, an unusual feat for that time. This meant Maria was also given the rare opportunity to progress right through to further education. Her intellect was strong, as was her passion. Though discouraged by tutors and society itself, she wanted to be a doctor, and so passed the relevant tests to gain a place on the course.

There is a funny little anecdote shared about her time studying. Due to the situation between men and women at the time, she wasn't allowed to attend the classes where they'd dissect a human body, as it was seen as well awkward/inappropriate for her to be exposed to the naked form (no matter how dead they may have been) around men. They didn't banish her totally from the experience though, she just had to do it on her own in the evenings.

She became a doctor, specialising in paediatrics and psychiatry, and fell in love, but again, due to the situation for women at the time, they decided not to marry as it would be expected that Maria would have to abandon her career. At that moment, she was not only super passionate about her work but she was also becoming pretty successful. The man she loved promised that they would be forever committed even if they weren't married and so they had a child together. Apparently, the pressure from his family got to him, though, and he ended up marrying another woman. Maria was understandably devastated and had to reluctantly employ a wet nurse to raise her son for the first few years as her mission for social action had begun to gain momentum.

Classroom/Research Lab

In 1906, following lots of research into childhood development and learning, she started her first school in Rome. The thing I really love about Maria Montessori is that she wanted to reach the kids that needed her. And because she came from a therapeutic background, she was all about helping children to find their way of being in the world, not about moulding them into 'something'. The first school she created was a place for children with specialist needs or challenging behaviour that had been written off as impossible to educate. They weren't welcome in mainstream education, so she created a school specifically for them, characterised by hands-on learning opportunities. The results were remarkable. These kids had been given up on before Maria found them, and yet there they were, calmly engaging, learning and developing way past what the system had deemed their level of ability to be. Another phenomenon that seemed to naturally arise from the approach was a feeling of responsibility within the children to take care of the school environment. Without being instructed to, they really respected and looked after their shared space.

Over the coming years, due to the success that she continued to highlight, more and more of these schools were created, starting in Italy and then developing across the world. Her work was not only benefiting the children involved but it was also enriching the fields of both education and therapeutics. There were instances where classrooms were made with glass walls for people to come and witness the method and study the new learnings arising about human development that were being revealed. I'm not sure how I feel about kids in a tank, but they apparently weren't disturbed by people witnessing them and continued to follow their flow.

Montessori schools are characterised by a balance of facilitated activity and self-direction. As opposed to focusing mainly on teaching, explorative learning is the main component. The environment is purposefully created and there are specialist learning materials in the space. Children are not separated by age group and have freedom to move around. They get to follow their interests and can work uninterrupted for hours on end. Though there is an externally created schedule for the day, there is choice within it. And there are no formal tests or examinations.

The world wars really put a plug in a lot of the progressive things that were opening up, like the work of Montessori and Steiner. By the 1920s, critics started to attack her approach and by the 1930s all of the Montessori schools in Italy were shut down. Not only that, Maria was exiled for her work and labelled as an Italian enemy. This led her to India where she lived for seven years. Her legal status meant she could not travel but she still managed to train 1,500 teachers during that time. Go on, lass! Italy later revoked her status and she was able to return to europe. In the late 1950s, Nancy McCormick Ramsbusch went to visit Maria and in perfect alignment with the progressive 60s culture, the schools resurged and continue to exist all over the world.

Maria was nominated for the Nobel Peace Prize three times, and rightly so. This woman was fiercely committed to children's rights and all her work rolled out from this central point. For this she was exiled but continued with her mission. She lived defiantly outside of the expectations of wider society and created huge ripples that still exist today.

Though there are many schools, very different approaches to the methodology exist because Montessori education is not patented. Anyone can use the name even if their setting strays far from what Maria's schools looked like. I met someone recently who enrolled their children in a Montessori school with high hopes but ended up disappointed as it didn't embody much of the method. Though the lack of patenting means the system is often watered down, it does mean that the schools are able to evolve with the times. Though criticised by some, technology is used in intentional ways within certain schools and there are even apps for educators. I feel there is a balance point where education philosophies can be protected but also able to progress with the times, in alignment with the world outside the classroom.

GREEN SCHOOL BALI

One of the more modern, well-known alternative schools started in Bali. In 2008, John and Cynthia Hardy, entrepreneurs and home educators, decided to open an international school with a radical twist. They felt deeply moved to educate young people about sustainability and empower the next generation of change-makers and eco-warriors. *Green School* is famous the world over with three more centres now opening in New Zealand, Mexico and South Africa.

Early on in my unintentional research journey, I visited the school in Bali and cried happy tears when I found it. The first thing to note when you enter Green School is it's phenomenal and sustainable architecture. Huge bamboo structures with spirals mirrored in nature, platforms, nests and wall-less classrooms make up the learning environment. The whole place vibrates with delight, built around and within the wild nature that existed on the land before they started building. A tropical jungle paradise.

When I visited, I was on a tour with prospective parents. As always, I ended up befriending two children and having all the fun alongside receiving crazy amounts of inspiration. We got to touch the huge crystal in the prayer garden, run through the 10ft musical bamboo pipes, say hello to chickens and other animals and generally have a whale of a time, whilst all the grown-ups offered the occasional frown to our noisy, distracting and playful behaviour. If only they had come and played with us! Whilst on that tour, the little girl handed me a seed (gotta love these psychic bambinos) and just before I left, there was a swarm of about a thousand dragonflies. Potent omens. Visiting Green School was an experience that not only inspired me to my core but also demonstrated that the dreams we have are possible and very much needed at this time.

Project-Based Learning

The school follows the track of *project-based learning*, which means every subject is taught through a specific assignment. This method is sometimes even applied in state schools and is a wonderful middle ground between radical and mainstream approaches to education. I recently learned that primary education in the UK was project-based not so many years ago but the control belt has sadly tightened since those days.

During my visit to Green School, the youngest children were raising chickens. They each had a chicken to take care of and would gather and sell their eggs to the local community. How's that for some integration? Real world learning! I literally fell to bits when I witnessed the eldest students' projects though. They had each designed and built their own bicycle! The main frame was bamboo and the rest of the elements were completely recycled materials. And they weren't clunky pieces of junk, either; not only were they fully functional, they were also really sleek and beautiful. Seriously cool! And obviously, the desire to create their own bicycle meant that everyone showed up to class - who wouldn't? As you can imagine, the level of technical skill and knowledge required to create a functioning bike is high and spans many different subject areas, but again, the motivation was there.

Within project-based models, demonstration of learning is through production. There are no tests, just a design brief and a (hopefully) finished product that has been successful or not.

Students learn in collaborative ways and a lot of the time teach themselves what they need to know to fulfil the assignment. Each project pushes exploration and learning within a multitude of different subject areas and the approach is *student-centred*. They enter a period of discovery, turning over many rocks to find the information they need to meet the project outline. There are taught 'lessons' around the brief but the curriculum is much broader, providing greater space for learners to follow their personal desire down rabbit holes that the present mainstream approach to education does not have the space to facilitate. According to Frank Zapper, *autocratic learning* (self-direction) is the key and, to me, that dude was pretty switched on. Teaching ourselves allows the information to integrate as we desire to know it for a greater purpose. Meaning is everything for humans, especially when it comes to drive.

Adults have more freedom within project-based learning initiatives as they are not tightly bound to a curriculum. They don't have to prove their ability to teach through high scores on standardised tests. They are autonomous creatives that get to pour their passion into designing a project to engage their students, creating a multifaceted, holistic learning experience. Teachers often co-create, too, cross-pollinating to create assignments where they each offer their subject knowledge to the pot. What a fulfilling environment for students and teachers alike.

There are formulated and expected learning outcomes within project-based learning models but there is also freedom and agency for young people. They are in control. As opposed to a pass or fail grade, they either sit back after a load of hard work and witness what they have created or they do not. Sometimes the project brief is a group piece of work, where young people learn about their own strengths and weaknesses and how they harmonise with the skills and limitations of their peers. Allowing young people responsibility and decision making within their learning experiences creates so many good things.

A huge body of theory in playwork critically examines the dependency upon adults presently embodied by children in the west. Children expect adults to sail in and fix problems, and grown-ups are very accustomed to doing this! 'Let me show you how' is something that reinforces a sense of worthiness in otherwise lost human beings. It also continues this weird dependent loop where kids grow into adults that need someone to push them/save them/fix them. Both children and adults are used to micromanagement within learning (and all other aspects of our lives and relationships!) but stepping back from that temptation truly allows the creative learning process to take place. When we engage with life and learning under our own steam, we get the space to discover and innovate.

Without the notion of pass/fail, the drive for creation is maintained better than it would be in a standard set up. The capacity for creativity is developed. "Okay, that didn't work, what needs to be tweaked so that it does? What do I need to learn? What skills do I need to develop in order to successfully create what I desire?" And if that is not a next level transferable life skill, I have no idea what is. The notion of failure is replaced with an open-ended creative drive that births, reflects, adjusts and rebirths.

Certain project-based learning schools, like *High Tech High* in California, have a public viewing at the end of the term. This provides another very relevant experience that would be expected in the workplace - producing something to a timeframe that will be analysed upon completion. You make the thing, then people see it. The assessment is the unveiling. "Is it functioning correctly? Does it represent the project outline?" The true 'test' is about how you feel about your creation when people see it. It's also interesting to note that there is no immediate reward within this approach, which in some ways makes it harder. This kind of education seems extremely relevant for the times, without being super far from the mainstream model.

Intentional Space

Alongside the inspirational project-based learning approach, the curriculum at Green School is created with specific intentions. As well as nurturing its pupils, it aims to develop a deep environmental consciousness within students, supporting them to live in harmony with the natural world. Every part of the curriculum is woven around this. We've spoken about the *hidden curriculum* of schooling, but our entire global reality could arguably be transmitting the idea of consumerism deep into our psyches with devastating consequences.

The world is increasingly governed by consumer industry, and I would say that the reason we get caught in the consumer trap which fuels said industry is due to deep unfulfillment. If the past few years of global lockdowns have taught us anything, it's about meaning. It didn't matter that we could still buy things and have them delivered the next day (and we did a lot of that!); we were in pain because we felt isolated and powerless. This isn't a new feeling for us humans. It's a strangely common experience of the world today and that is why I believe the events in our collective experience are crescendo-ing now. We are unfulfilled, our lives lack meaning, we believe we can do nothing to change it and we get caught in all manner of traps and trips to dissociate from these feelings. At some point we have to feel it, grieve it and reform ourselves. My own experience has taught me that the outer world will keep turning up the situations in our lives until we face our feelings, let them crush us and then experience the inevitable rebirth that follows, rebirthing our collective reality accordingly.

In the 1960s, Martin Seligman did some pretty questionable experiments with animals to explore a theory he called *learned helplessness*. When we learn through repeated experience that we are powerless, we essentially give up, even when presented with situations that we can influence. Whether on purpose or accidentally, mainstream schooling repeatedly serves us the 'this is just the way it is, so get used to it' narrative. Fostering the idea of 'we can and are changing things' is something painstakingly missing from school and life. Young people that make a stand learn very quickly that the overarching power of the adult world will either enable them or crush them, whether in their bedroom or in the world at large. But the beauty of Green School is that it is growing activists on purpose. Not just through curriculum, either; it embodies what it teaches. Alongside the biodiesel school bus, Green School provided the only recycling plant on the island of Bali at the time of my visit. The young people constantly witness the way their institution is changing the world for the better, demonstrating that collective action is powerful and that it matters, that individual action is powerful and that it matters.

In 2018, Greta Thunberg skipped school and sat outside Swedish Parliament with a sign that said, 'School Strike for Climate'. In

March 2019, 1.5 million students protested alongside her, and the following September 4 million people across the world went on strike for climate change. I still sob about things like this. One person. One voice. One action that rolled into huge action. Greta has been bullied and projected upon constantly but she is doing more for the world than all the haters put together. She made people think. She made people consider their impact. And that is what creates change. I behave differently in the world because of Greta. We are responsible for our decisions; it's not simply in the hands of politicians. We need more Gretas. And Green School exists to birth them.

Young people at the school grow up understanding the very real situation we are facing on the planet as a result of modern living, but they are also given the tools and knowledge to be a skilful group of people pushing in the opposite direction. It's bloody beautiful! If schools were institutions that intended to develop and condition humans into being Earth protectors and super conscious beings, I'd be much more on board (but my radical streak won't ever sit well with coercion and force, even if it is for 'the good of all').

Green School was set in the most glorious natural environment. There is quite obviously a huge pull to create schools and projects in 'developing' countries. The whole thing is much cheaper, there is probably going to be less input from the government and the climate is usually more reliably warm which enables a different kind of learning community. But there is something that hurts me within this dynamic. I've attended many retreats and gatherings and visited spiritual communities all over the world. These experiences, though fundamentally life-changing, were often run by white western people, giving us a taste of paradise where we could be waited on hand and foot by local people in a seemingly heavenly temple space built for a fraction of the price it would cost on western land. There's this skin-crawling trend where western 'conscious' community is overlayed upon an existing (usually very spiritual) culture. It's exploitative. It's messed up. And it's the new shade of colonialism.

Though in some ways it's a repeat of the same pattern, Green School has done fairly well in connecting the school to the local community. Alongside scholarships and the recycling plant, the school interacted with the local village regularly and I saw many Balinese workers on site. I'm not sure what they were paid, though. And I don't know the solution for this. Part of me wants to say, "Build in your own communities on the land you were born upon." But I recognise that funding is a very real issue. For instance, to buy a little piece of land here in the UK is a heck of a lot of money, and the government is like a very controlling and interfering mother which makes it hard to create revolutionary things. But what's worth doing is hard.

You'd think that establishing a school in Bali would mean it is more accessible financially, but that couldn't be further from the truth! I can imagine the teachers are on high-end western wages and, as you've heard, the place is fan-bloody-tastic, but the fees for Green School make it very exclusive. Enrolment alone costs £3566.14 (at the time on writing, in 2021) and cost for one year's tuition is between £5636.55 and £14506.19. Sadly, only super privileged young people get the opportunity to receive the moulding to become environmental protectors and world changers, in a similar fashion to the private schools in the UK, like Eton that seem to be a direct track to conservative politics. But, giving credit where it is due, Green School does offer a large number of scholarship places to young Balinese people. I'm not sure if this is a legal requirement from Bali officials or something that the school decided to create for themselves, but it does offset the prickliness somewhat.

Green School is a phenomenal place. And I would love to see more environmentally conscious and project-based learning opportunities integrate into mainstream schooling, so that all kids can have the chance to grow in such a nourishing way.

SUMMERHILL

It is now time to introduce you to yet another one of my favourite humans. The man, the legend, the revolutionary Scottish Victorian, Alexander Sutherland Neill. This man's work was at one time compulsory reading when schoolteachers were passing through college. But as teaching and life settled back into conformity following the progressive 60s and 70s, his work and ideologies became once again stuck in an echo chamber, though the school he created in 1921 lives on to this day.

Neill was born in the 1880s not long after Maria Montessori. I was really surprised to find out when he was born - his ideas are radical now, in our modern age of progressive perspective, never mind in the Victorian era. Being beaten into submission and compliance was the name of the game back then. Subsequently, he was raised in a very strict environment with a schoolteacher father and always struggled to meet the expectations placed upon him. Neill was forced into his dad's classroom as a teaching assistant but hated it, perhaps because he didn't feel comfortable embodying the authoritarian energy of his father, which teaching was (and is) often correlated with.

In his mid-twenties, he went to university and for a while flirted with the idea of being a journalist. I mean, this man can write! But destiny took the reins and when he was deemed unfit for military service, he was appointed head teacher at a local school. In this role, he called the shots and was able for the first time to throw out what he didn't like about schooling, relaxing the dynamic between pupil and teacher and emphasising creativity, encouraging his students to question the wisdom of the day. As a result of his approach, he was invited to work at a progressive school in Germany and began focusing more on 'problem children'.

He understood what models such as *non-violent communication* (NVC) are bringing to our awareness now - out of balance behaviour is simply a cry for love. And Alexander knew the remedy from the word go: love them! When the progressive school was forced to relocate, the local community which now surrounded got rather prickly about its wild ways, so Neill moved the school again in 1924 to an estate called Summerhill in England. In 1927, the school, still named Summerhill, moved location to Leiston in Suffolk where it has remained ever since. It was the first democratic school and inspired many more to birth across the world.

Alexander recognised that when adults allied with young people as opposed to against them, they felt heard and validated, and more often than not, 'problem' behaviour subsided. When children feel loved and approved of, they feel safe. He didn't believe in naughtiness, only in unhappiness, and said his role (and the role of every educator) was to cure unhappiness. To discover the unmet need and remedy it. I remember when I first read Neill's words. I cried so hard. He believed in children's innate goodness and understood that, when left untampered with, they become who they are meant to be - themselves. He was all about happiness over achievement and saw fulfilment as the ultimate goal. Education for him was not about forced learning; it was a space to develop personality and character. He also believed that externalised authority could not possibly create free adults and that young people needed to have opportunities to explore their own needs, wants and desires through being able to listen to themselves.

Democratic Education

The foundation of Summerhill and Neill's radical education methods was freedom. Freedom to be oneself, freedom to have influence over the things in life that concern us, freedom to be and freedom to love. Though there were taught lessons at the school, voluntary attendance was the key. The subjects and classroom set up was pretty traditional, but the difference was <u>consent</u>. If children wanted to go to class, they attended; if they didn't feel drawn, they didn't go. They were free to govern themselves and their time in the way they decided to. No pressure, no guilt trips, no 'you're free to choose, but you should make the grown-up and mature decision and be a good girl or boy'. No manipulation script. It's such a strange phenomenon in childhood; our time is not our own, our experience is not our own. We must live through another's schedule and meet another's expectations. Traditional childhood is a very disempowering experience. John Holt suggested in 1974 that "childhood is a prison that must be escaped from", yet here we find Alexander in the 1920s, beating the same drum and letting young people roam free.

Now, the expectation - because we don't trust children - is that this must have had some pretty dire consequences. How would children ever be motivated? Get anything done? Achieve anything? But the phenomenon that the school revealed again and again was that when behaviour is intrinsically motivated, when the desire to 'do' is about one's own agenda, students fully engage with what they choose. There is no resistance. And because there is no notion of 'failure,' there is freedom to grow at one's own pace without judgment or shame. Though there were no formal examinations at the school (notice the theme in all these 'alternative' spaces?), young people could study for exams if that is what they wanted to do. The whole notion of 'they don't know what they want because they are children' is because children have usually had no opportunity to explore what it is that they want to do. This is highlighted in the present with university education – only a handful of people graduate with a degree which leads to a career in the subject matter, and even less end up feeling fulfilled in their role. It's also important to point out, as Alexander often did, that we have not cured the world of anything; education hasn't healed our issues. The diseases still exist, we just have medication to offset the effects. The wars, world hunger, environmental destruction and criminality are all still here.

Neill in some ways feared the influence of the outside world and needed to find a way to protect his vision. He was unwilling to compromise, as for him that would mean also compromising the children, so he made the school a boarding school. The kids came and lived together during term time. It made it easier for the school philosophy to unfold without criticism or input from the outside world. He openly recognised the school as a bubble but he wasn't trying to create societal change; he was creating change for the young people in his care. He created a living, breathing community where adults and children co-existed and created culture together.

Summerhill was created to facilitate autonomy through democracy. Each week there was a *general school meeting*, the most fundamental component of the school. The chairman of the meeting was a student and rotated each week, with the present chairman selecting their predecessor. During meetings, the whole community would gather to discuss the week, make decisions, share complaints and cover whatever was on the collectively created agenda. Everyone could share their opinions, question, counter argue or suggest alternatives. Once things had been discussed, a vote would follow to decide upon next steps. The democratic vote decided everything; from the introduction of new opportunities or projects to the implications of breaking a rule or crossing someone's boundaries. Every member of the community had one vote, from the 5-year-old girl to Alexander Neill. All were equally valid and important. The only elements of the school that the children did not have influence over were the bedrooms, food, bills and staffing. What a powerful, embodied experience of democracy! I wonder how different our relationships with political systems would be if childhood taught us that our voice counts and has influence?

All relationships at Summerhill were underpinned by respect. Two-sided respect. Often, people assume that Neill's philosophy of freedom meant unruly kids trampling upon one another, but Alexander always stressed **'freedom WITHOUT license.'** Do as you please until it affects another person without their consent. In the modern day, I guess we would call this love with boundaries. Neill often noted the different flavour of conflict when all parties are equals. The disagreement would be about a 'thing' and wouldn't result in character annihilation or become about what is 'right or wrong'; it was simply a boundary issue that needed to be discussed and rectified.

Summerhill had a huge rule book that the community themselves created in response to incidents. "If 'x' happens, then 'y' is the agreed upon punishment." Most often the punishment would be a pocket money fine. As we've all grown through the distortion of externalised authority figures, the idea of rules can feel limiting. But these agreed upon commitments were essentially a map of the boundaries of people within the space. Always open to question, reinterpretation and adaption, an ideal representation of how to do relationship. As we grow and change, so too do our boundaries, and if we are to have conscious relationships then the discussion of our boundaries needs to be an open-ended conversation.

People or groups often become authority figures through rank or privilege, making decisions on behalf of larger communities, yet at Summerhill, everyone was part of the authority. Neill often noted the ways in which this created a strong culture of trust and responsibility; the threat of community condemnation was incredibly influential. If you weren't respectful of the collectively agreed upon rules, you were taken to trial in front of the whole school and everyone was a part of what happened next. Your actions would become public knowledge. The consequences would not be discussed in an office in secret but publicly by your peers; the teachers, students and/or work colleagues.

Especially unusual in the 1920s was the lack of religious indoctrination at Summerhill. No ideologies were forcibly implanted but there were no restrictions, either. People were free to follow any belief system they desired. Neill studied psychology and provided one-to-one therapeutic sessions for pupils throughout his time at the school, but this eventually didn't sit right with him. He was openly very influenced by the waves of the 60s and 70s and really got into a lot of the progressive thinking of the time, but later dropped some of the ideas when his experience, especially with the kids, didn't reveal the notions as truth. If you read his books, you'll witness the ways his ideas change. Certain things he once championed later become renounced and people have criticised him for this. What I see, though, is a very real and reflective person receiving the perceived wisdom of his day, combining these ideas with his own revelations and allowing the two to distil over time into his own continually updating truth.

Summerhill still exists, in pretty much the same way as it always has, hosting around 75 pupils aged between five and seventeen. Most of the students board but there are day pupils too. The headteacher is Zoë Readhead, Alexander's daughter. She was born after Summerhill was in full swing, grew up in the school and then took over her dad's legacy. Sadly, just like at Green School, the fees make it very exclusive - it's between £8000 - £15000 per year (do bear in mind that this is for boarding too). The reality is that if you want to start a school in the UK that isn't following the national curriculum, the government aren't gonna fund you. It's just how it is.

When I visited Summerhill, I was blown away. I attended a conference to celebrate the 100 year anniversary of the school. The grounds and facilities are beautiful and you can feel the ways in which everyone involved is fully committed to children and their rights. The best bit, as always, was meeting some of the young people that attended. Unique, free-thinking beings that felt safe and confident in their individuality. It made my heart sing. The talks were profound, too. Whenever I witness people talk (or write) passionately about children and their rights, I sob. Y'know, the kind of teary convulsions where your heart explodes with joy and your eyes can't help but throw out salty warm rivers. When you feel enamoured and inspired, and just **know** that humanity is going to be okay 'cause things like this are happening.

There were record levels of rain for August when I visited Summerhill. The UK is famous for rain, so I'm sure you can imagine just how much rain we were facing. It knocked the power out in the local village on my way down, but I just had to get there. The camping aspect of the conference was hilarious. I had recently bought an incredibly cute little tipi tent. It was definitely not built for rain – madness, really, to attempt UK camping in such a thing but it was so darn pretty! It was blue and white with birdies flying through flowers on the side. I decorated it like a little fairy den with lights and flags, and the little girl within me was ultimately fulfilled inside it when the sun was shining. But the sun didn't join the conference. The rain hammered the whole time we were there and on the final night, I awoke to find my airbed floating. My 3am solution to the rising water levels inside my tent was to repeatedly stab the floor with a fork. There I was, soaking wet, floating on an inflatable mattress in the dark, ripping holes in the floor of my tent with cutlery.

I left Summerhill with my story. As everyone does.

The discovery of democratic education had the same kind of impact upon my life and perspectives that playwork had delivered all those years previously. My comprehension of what was possible up-levelled again, another destiny activation moment where my heart fire was switched up a notch. I didn't know that a child-centred approach to education that wasn't based upon manipulation, existed. But this was only the tip of the iceberg. And as you'll come to see, there are many variants of this profound model now in existence.

PART 3

(the research)

THE BACKDROP

Class and Socio-Economic Status

I was led back to academia whilst staying in the Blue Mountains in Australia (I'll share that magical tale later). I decided I wanted to do a research paper about democratic education. I wanted to understand Summerhill from an education perspective and on a political level, too, but I didn't want to study white privileged kids. Not because I have anything against them, it's just that if the children I'm studying have both parents, a comfortable amount of money and secure lives, it's hard to distinguish between the influence of their homelives and the impact of their educational experiences.

Class is something close to my heart. For our international readers, it feels important to let you know that the UK, and England specifically, is not just rolling hills and well-spoken colonists. There is a deep discrepancy between socio-economic classes, as I'm sure exists everywhere. There are very specific layers of wealth which give rise to very different experiences of life.

Both sides of my family were born into poverty. My grandmother's family used to trade in their best clothes every week to have some money to float over the weekend. The kids would run round after the coal man to collect the bits he dropped on his rounds to try and keep warm in the winter. They'd get new clothes once a year for Whitsuntide; the rest of the time they'd put cardboard in their holey shoes. My grandad was thoroughly rejected by teachers and classmates alike for being the poorest of the poor and he suffered greatly, as, unlike my grandmother, love wasn't freely available in his home to keep him feeling warm and secure. These experiences were not uncommon in Bradford. I am from a working-class city, and though the times have moved on, poverty within the working class is still very real. It has pretty much transitioned now from *absolute poverty* (unable to afford food and keep oneself warm) to *relative poverty* (only able to meet basic needs).

Another point to briefly mention here is that at the height of the Industrial Revolution, Bradford's mills were world famous for textiles and many workers were shipped from overseas for cheap labour. A large proportion of these workers were from Pakistan and a lot of families settled in the city. As is always the way with political agenda and media distortions, instead of poverty uniting the citizens of Bradford, the 'downfall of Bradford' has been blamed upon the influx of international people. And thus is the way with systematic oppression; the system operates invisibly and people draw their own conclusions, usually pointing fingers at one another.

Both of my parents managed to do 'well' for themselves, which seemed to be the way of the baby boomers. They got to ride the explosions of the housing market and were the generation that rose following the war times. I had a beautiful childhood in a semi-urban environment. I was loved, I felt safe, I was always encouraged to be myself. My mum was a phenomenal human and to my awareness money was never an issue. In my teens, however, life as I knew it crashed and burned. I was taken under the wing of an amazing single mum; her son was my boyfriend at the time. I lived with them on a council estate (social housing) for several years and it was here that I discovered the meaning of community; the limitations, challenges and superpowers that come with having a very limited amount of money and how class privilege manifests.

My parents embodied the energy of 'trying to be someone', working hard to embody a role or status in society to demonstrate success. And to be honest, I feel that striving added to my mum's early transition. My friends on the estate had an embodied rejection of authority and a 'I am who I am' identity that offered itself to a kind of liberation, alongside all the limitations of living in poverty. There was no pretence or bullshit and an ability to say no that made me feel really safe. And people took care of one another.

When I got older and began transitioning into the world of alternative health, spirituality, education and culture, I found myself within a very white, middle-class environment. I lived in a village that had the heroin issues gentrified out of it and was filled with people wanting to change themselves and the world by living 'consciously'. I loved it! The people I met during these times were and are amazing, taking great consideration with their children's physical, emotional and mental health, conscious of what their kids were being fed on every level. But as was the case when I lived in Glastonbury, it was a bubble. Privileged people living privileged lives. Living really gently and intentionally but preserving that existence by closing the door to the surrounding community and its issues.

At present, I live in one of the poorest areas of Bradford with the highest population of people with Pakistani heritage, and it truly feels like home. My heart belongs in India and I see the similarities between the cultures mixed beautifully with the gritty, shining heart of Bradford. My experiences of life have given me quite a unique perspective upon collective issues that influence everything, especially my feelings and intentions around social action.

Though Summerhill set my heart on fire, I was looking to find a place that would let me examine and explore self-directed, democratic education without being heavily influenced (and therefore somewhat skewed) by class and race privilege. My Master of Research (MRes) proposal was accepted and I found myself back in university. From afar. Planted in Goa. Living the best life that my reality could offer. It was pretty hilarious looking back on it. I would spend the hottest points of the day in this big internet café on my laptop in the middle of Arambol's bustling high street, somehow riding the inevitable power cuts that would close everything down regularly for an indefinite amount of time. I was reading a crazy amount of literature and drinking a ridiculous amount of chai, but at night I was dancing ecstatically under the stars with soul tribe and my Greek lover, in front of the glistening ocean. What was I just chatting about privilege?

I quickly discovered that there were democratic schools inspired by Summerhill all over the world. But the familiar obstacle came up every time: astronomical fees. Somehow, I discovered the *charter school movement* in the USA. Seemingly, the government in certain states was offering funding to alternative schools. There was a set amount of money for every child's education, paid to the provision the family chose, whether state or private. I later discovered whilst sharing a taxi with a couple that happened to be mainstream teachers in the US that there was a downside to this. As each state had a specific amount of funding in their education budget, struggling schools that depended upon extra funding to support more vulnerable students had to go without. Funding alternative schools meant that underprivileged kids were having an even worse time (mega sigh).

Before I learned that piece, I'd found two democratic 'schools' in the state of California, both seemingly very accessible and inclusive. Their websites made me cry tears of joy, which as you've probably learned by now is my intuitive marker, and so I contacted them. Before I knew it, my tickets were booked and I was on my way.

Being a Researcher

Doing research with children is fraught with difficulties. In the run up to any kind of academic research, you're taught to really examine your position as 'researcher' and be aware of your influence in the space and with the people you're talking to. This is amplified 1000% when it comes to children. Children are conditioned deeply to impress adults as we hold the power, and so in a research sense, it's hard to decipher what is naturally occurring and what is happening in response to your presence. I did manage to hide in corners and go under the radar at points, witnessing some really awesome things. There were also moments that I was full-on inside the experience gathering solid data. Very meta.

Not only that but I've got dreadlocks, piercings and tattoos, which brings its own kind of influence, for adults and children alike. It's really obvious that I'm a liberal person. The topic I was researching also demonstrated my passions and so it was probably easy to guess what I was 'hoping' to hear and see. If you've not already gathered, I'm also rubbish at plugging my emotions (and oppose ideas that I should!), so if something moves me, I can't stop a huge smile appearing or tears popping out of my face.

What I want to convey here is that one side of me is very well suited to being a researcher. People feel safe with me and thus are really honest. I'm a good listener and thrive upon witnessing people in their truth. But at the same time, my appearance and energy could very easily influence people to share with me what they think I want to hear. This is where Feminism swings into the picture again, though (yay).

Instead of the traditional idea, which sees the researchers' influence as something negative, Feminist methodology argues that actually having a 'real person' researcher can create more safety and thus more depth within what is expressed. Researchers are often embodying a weird superiority thing because they're apparently the clever one doing the investigating. Yuck! But if a person shows up authentically and from a more horizontal (and respectful) place, that dynamic shifts somewhat. And the other Feminist piece in all of this is about letting emotion come back into academia. Instead of trying to strip the empathy out of research to make it more valid, the argument is that greater levels of empathy create a richer picture. Research, especially sociological research, is meant to expose social issues with a view to overcome them, <u>because</u> we care.

Another one of the reasons I'm much happier writing a book than a thesis is that I can write as me. I can express my opinions. I can be playful. I can start sentences with 'and'. I can use curse words. I can put full stops in weird places. I can write in the same way I talk and think. I'd be damned if I did any of that in academia! I mean, have you ever read a piece of academic writing? Even if the ideas and theories are super progressive and profound, the clunky, sterilised, 'I use big words and I'm well clever' language is classist, elitist and a brain-crunching mission to read. And it is the most recognised and validated expression of information. Feminist research theory is trying to unshackle the validation of knowledge from the hands of the institution. So many reasons to be grateful for Feminism.

One final, brief note here: for the purpose of ease, I refer to the settings I visited during my research as 'schools'. They don't really fulfil the criteria (and to be honest, they are the antithesis) but I was at a loss as to what word to use, so take the term *school* with a pinch of salt.

Home Education

I didn't understand how funding worked for the schools I was visiting until I landed in the US. The children were all registered as home-educated and accessed funding through a charter school cluster **if** they progressed in correlation to a national average, demonstrated by online tests that families had to submit. The responsibility for this was left in the hands of the parents so the schools could function in alignment with the self-directed philosophy. If parents wanted a funded place, they had to make sure the tests were passed.

Home education is becoming increasingly popular and is a blanket term for educating children from home. To differentiate from the mainstream approach, the majority of parents I've spoken to favour the term *home education* instead of *homeschooling,* but I will use the terms interchangeably. There is a vast spectrum of approaches - some parents follow the national curriculum and have a very structured format, mirroring the traditional school day. Another of my favourite humans is a professional triathlon athlete I met and fell in love with in Bali who spent years sailing round the world with her partner, raising their children whilst living in the wilds of the ocean. She is an absolute diamond of being. Though their lifestyle was insanely colourful and radical, school on their little boat happened in a pretty traditional and formal way. And that totally worked for their free-spirited life!

Worldschooling is more recent phenomenon. You hit the road with your family and travel round the world. No official schooling, just experiencing life and all the richness that comes with it. For some, like my friend in Bali, there is a 'school day' and an official routine that happens pocketed within different cultures of the world. For others, its closer to unschooling - no formal intervention, just playtime on the road.

The decision to homeschool is ripe with challenges and difficulties, often foremostly from the position of funding. It is generally a full-time job without financial reward, meaning that many of these parents/carers have to survive on minimal income. Another challenge is around demonstrating the validity of what is being taught and learned at home to the local authority. The influence and involvement of The State is argued to be about preventing neglect. There have been a handful of cases where bad things were going down. But most of the time, people are taking their kids out of the system through choice because they want to give them a different experience. I'm leaving my conspiracy hat on the floor for this book.

There are many reasons why people choose to home educate. For some, it's about creating a different kind of education for their children, while others don't like the school environment. Some homeschool for religious reasons, then there are the children that have been kicked out of mainstream education and have nowhere to go. Let's also not forget that many families were forced to educate from home in recent years due to the lockdowns we experienced.

Homeschooling provides a greater potential to flexibly meet the needs of each child. Instead of one approach for many children, there's scope to personalise it. But taking risks with our children is something we are heavily conditioned against. I mean, every man and his dog has opinions about how we should interact with, feed, educate and parent children. It can be an absolute minefield. Nobody wants to be the person that made a huge mistake and fudges their kids up. Again, though, let's just pause for a reality check. Our parents fudge us up. It's kind of part of the process. And, as you've read, we have been experimenting with alternative education models for a long time now with wonderful results.

I've struggled with home education as it often doesn't give young people the opportunity to experience childhood culture. They are with adults or their siblings most of the time, so there's not that awesome opportunity to diversify through meeting and developing relationships with other young people that have had different experiences of life. Though school for me was not a stimulating or inspiring place, my friends were. Having a massive group of young people around me all the time was the highlight of those years. It was the **biggest** learning piece. And I fear that without that experience, we're robbing children of something really key.

Self-Directed Learning and Unschooling

In *'Deschooling Society'* (1971), Ivan Illich (the radical priest and social critic referenced earlier) presents multiple ways in which schooling forms our mentality, creating the basis for power distortions and the corrupted motivations for consumer society. John Holt was very much on the same page. He was a fierce advocate for children's rights and published a number of books that have arguably become 'must reads' for homeschooling families. His background, as most people in this field share, was in formalised, mainstream education. It was John that coined the term *unschooling*; a hands-off approach where learning is led by a child's curiosity in a very informal and self-directed way. Learning through living life without it being a 'set up' learning experience. In a similar way to Alexander Neill, Holt was a person that trusted the innate learning mechanisms within every individual. He didn't get on with mainstream schools and frequently criticised their coercive nature, highlighting that they often do more harm than good and believing that the liberation of humanity will come through freedom from schooling.

One of the more limiting beliefs that came through school for me was about creativity. When I 'did art' at school I wasn't ever any good at drawing from my mind. When I left at 16, I was genuinely convinced that I wasn't a creative person. Even though I would cut and colour my hair in crazy ways, had a funky and individual dress sense, was able to create awesome little home spaces, doodled constantly in notebooks, spent my weekends moving my body to crazy beats and could put words together and make magic, I couldn't draw 'properly' and therefore, I wasn't creative. And not only that, because 'I'm not creative' was running the show in my life, I refused to even try. Eventually, in my twenties, I started to unravel, had my creative awakening and shed the conditioned ideas and beliefs around creativity that I'd soaked up from school. *The Artists Way'* (1992) by Julia Cameron is an incredible workbook for unlocking our innate creativity. Get it on your list! As I kicked the inner critic out of the driving seat, I started to develop a relationship with my creative self and even began to enjoy the experience of being a novice in certain art forms. I found joy in simply playing. I know I'm not the only one that came out of school with a heap of false ideas about myself and my abilities that continued to limit me once I left the institution.

I heard a really interesting guy talk at a conference once called Sugarta Mitra. He and his colleagues worked as researchers at a university in India and their campus was next to a slum. In 1999, they decided to do an experiment to explore how young people learn, especially in regard to computer technology which was becoming an integral component of modern life. Their experiment, *'A Hole in the Wall',* involved inserting a computer into the wall between the slum and the university for the kids to use without any instructions. They wanted to see what would happen. Their discoveries were fascinating. Through exploration, the young people taught themselves how to use the functions of the PC. They figured out how to send emails, open web browsers and programs and switch the thing on and off. The full shebang of what a late 90s computer was able to offer. They named the different functions and components of the machine, like the mouse, with words that became a shared language, initiating one another into what they'd discovered. It was a community experience. From this, the researchers concluded many things, including that children learn best when able to explore with one another and that self-directed learning works. I love this piece of research so much!

Dr Peter Gray is another very cool dude, a pillar of inspiration and support for many people that are choosing to do things differently with children's education. Peter is a researcher and scholar who has come to play and self-directed education through psychology, conducting fascinating research into the way humans learn when self-directed. Utterly devoted to enabling social change through 'proving' the validity of the hands-off approach within the institution, alongside his own research he also hosts a peer support group for academic theorists that are researching self-directed learning. He is doing really important work for the field and children alike! His book '*Free to Learn*' (2013) has been pivotal for numerous parents and educators reframing the ways they see learning, education and their role with children in relation to those elements. He created an organisation called the *Alliance for Self-Directed Education,* a network of people doing awesome things in the field of unschooling. The website hosts a fantastic collection of free resources.

Peter's research from 2010 revealed that around 10% of homeschooling families identified themselves as *unschooling*. When asked to describe what unschooling meant to them, certain themes came through strongly; no curriculum, no tests and the freedom for young people to pursue their own interests. Unschooling parents believe that true learning happens when kids are allowed to follow what interests and inspires them. And because they remain in the driving seat of their experiences and haven't been controlled or taught that it's okay to control others, they're also better able to navigate relationships. The foundational belief within unschooling is that learning is happening constantly, naturally and that life itself is education. I must say, my research and experience aligns with this notion. The school of life has and continues to teach me much more than any institution!

One of the biggest challenges when embodying such an alternative approach to childrearing and learning is about what the neighbours think (and say!). Friends, family members and 'professionals' often subtly or overtly suggest that unschooling damages or neglects children in some way. We live in such a funny world of judgment when it comes to social norms. I'm all for critical thinking, but what comes with that is the necessity to research both sides of the equation. So often, people disregard or attack controversial ideas without investigation and study. And the same can be said for the opposite stance; many people adopt alternative ideologies without thorough investigation. Maybe this tendency is also a result of our schooling experiences? All the ways we have been taught to put our power in another's hands to guide us toward 'truth'.

There is also a deconditioning or *deschooling* process we have to go through to get on board with self-directed learning. On a conscious level, we might 'get it' and feel truly aligned with the idea that we don't need to push for growth to happen. But as most of us spent our most formative years moving through traditional schooling, the imprint is strong and reinforced by modern society. To talk about theories and ideas is one thing, but when the kids haven't desired to learn to read yet and their cousins in mainstream school have, the doubts pour in and all the old beliefs and ideas come to the surface.

It's such a remarkable thing, this conditioned mind we have. We might fully believe that we no longer want to follow or adhere to the prescribed ideas we've been indoctrinated by but the conditioned response, and essentially the fear, often cannot be overridden by thought alone. It's a practice which involves diving deep into ourselves, feeling our feelings and rewiring our minds. I can read all the books and have 'a-ha' moments left, right and centre, but the reality is that change only comes when I'm confronted with a familiar situation and instead of jumping to the action I've taken time and time again, I pause, facing and feeling all that fear and make a different choice. Taking an alternative route from conditioning is the ultimate challenge for humans in all realms of our lives.

Home educating in general also presents a huge challenge for parents. If you are devoting all your time and energy to your kids, it's near on impossible to pursue your own path or generate income outside of that. This is where community becomes essential. Anarchist networks, where nobody is above anyone else and people are simply gathering to share and co-create, can remedy these challenges but human relationships are hard and complicated. We haven't collectively arrived at a place where we can relate maturely and so community collaborations are often very difficult. I feel this is why we tend to lean on hierarchical models. With the right tools engrained into culture, however, as we will witness in due course, there is space for relational learning to happen on the job. Building community is about evolving the ways we relate, and by heck, I'd say that's the most important thing we need to work on as a collective.

The unschooling, hands-off and self-directed approach isn't suitable for every child, especially when it comes to neurodiversity (there's a chapter coming up on this), but the same can be said for the mainstream approach to education. As I've said before and will say again, it is impossible for a single approach to meet the needs of every child. I'm not calling for a reformation which shifts from one approach to another. I want us to diversify. The beauty of homeschooling is that there is more opportunity to do that; personalising, tweaking and giving space to meet the ever-changing needs and interests of each kid.

This opportunity is reflected in the legislative loophole that home education has existed within for many years in the UK. But as mentioned if successful, the proposed 'Schools Bill' may force families to prove children's learning. When human beings are growing organically, we develop at different rates in different areas. It drives me potty that in instances such as walking and talking we operate in surrender to this drive whilst then, just a few years later, we demand that children develop other skills such as reading and writing at a time we've deemed as appropriate. Self-directed families are going to have to get creative to ninja around this legislation if it does land in the UK. I've seen some inspirational ways to demonstrate development that might help with this which I'll introduce a little later.

The Research Begins

I was being naïve when I thought that funded places would mean I'd be interacting with young people that hadn't been given an array of tickets to success in their life. Though there were a couple, the majority of kids I met during my research were from loving homes and progressive parents. Which is great! It seems obvious now but I hadn't considered how much privilege a person must have to consider alternative education. None of this discounts what comes in the following chapters, it just feels important to say.

My research was about self-directed education so both the schools I visited adhered to this philosophy. I asked the eldest kid to define what self-directed meant to him and he said, "You choose your own path." The young people were in the driving seat of their experience, choosing what they did with their day and the only authority was the power of the collective. But the schools were different in approach and set up.

One was closely aligned with the *Sudbury* model. Sudbury Valley school was established in 1968 by a group of people in Massachusetts in the States. Sudbury schools follow the democratic process in pretty much the same way as Summerhill but have a completely hands-off approach, like unschooling. Nothing is 'offered' other than the physical environment: no lessons, sessions or workshops. There is no formal learning intervention unless the young people ask for it which gives space for some pretty phenomenal things to develop. The school I visited ran from a church hall with multiple rooms and a big outdoor space. There were about 20 kids in attendance between four and 14 years old with four adults. The surrounding area of this school to me felt like the 'America' I knew from movies. Little houses in rows that looked the same, neat little lawns with mailboxes on the edge and big cars in the driveways.

The second school I visited was in a sleepy hippy town. Little indie shops and cafes surrounded by mountains and a plethora of spiritual adventures on offer. It was a little different to traditional democratic models as it was an *Agile Learning Centre (ALC)*. Seeded in 2012 and established in 2013, Manhattan Free School was the first ALC. Arthur Brock, a software guy, was brainstorming with Thomas Parker, a staff member of the Manhattan Free School. They realised they could streamline the whole democratic education model using tools created for agile software development that Arthur was well-versed in. These systems from the tech world were created to tap into a group's creative potential, enable swift problem solving and support collaboration to produce high quality software. In ALC schools, these systems facilitate children's participation and streamline the democratic process to create community culture. The ALC I visited offered a rich program of workshops and classes that the young people could choose to attend or not, which again, allowed some pretty phenomenal things to be lived. Half the week the students were younger (up to 11 years old) and the rest of the time was for older kids (11+). There were around 50 young people on site each day, along with six mentors and numerous other adults that came to facilitate workshops or support the space.

Arriving in the States was quite an initiation for me! I went from wearing no shoes and floating round in the dusty heat of India to landing in the epitome of the west. Everything was so big. The food, the vehicles, the space, the wealth. I was naturally losing my s**t a bit but I have a deep connection to and trust for my intuition, so I just kept surrendering. Once I arrived at the schools, I stopped spinning out and it all made sense.

Though my research was about self-directed education, the majority of the coming chapters examine elements that could be found or created in any kind of education setting, even in mainstream schools. I'm not here to tell you how to educate or present you with a curriculum to follow. I'm here to inspire you through sharing the aspects of my research that made me scratch my noggin and the parts that made my heart sing. What follows are things I feel (with my geeky, rabbit hole, education theorist and children's rights activist hats on simultaneously) are the most important things to consider whether you are choosing to home educate, exploring alternative settings, setting up your own school, wanting to switch up your classroom culture or even just musing upon how to offset some of the more dodgy aspects of mainstream schooling. As adults, no matter how 'deschooled' we may be, permitting childhood freedom in a culture that doesn't believe in innate moral and developmental capacities can be fraught with fears, but it is my hope that what I have seen and lived might help your white knuckles to chill out a bit (or give you something to lean on when well-intentioned friends and family question your decisions).

Oh, and the upcoming chapters aren't in order of significance or anything like that. All of the following are equally important.

THE ENVIRONMENT

Mainstream environments for kids are usually pretty sterile and extremely controlled. Gosh, I don't do well in places like that. I am a fully-fledged fidgeter. I need to be able to get up, move around and follow my own flow. It's so strange that we've created places where this is deemed to be misbehaviour! When children are taught to sit still and supress the desire to interact, they learn that life is a cage and the creative urge must be ignored. But if they can follow their curiosity and tinker when their interest stimulates them, they learn that they are an empowered part of the world.

Green School was an amazing representation of what is possible with purposefully designed space. If we have unlimited resources and funding, we can create awesome things. But the reality is that visionaries rarely have bags of cash. Start-ups often struggle for resources and have to adopt spaces and adapt accordingly. Though physical space is important, there's a lot more to it. From the opportunities on offer to the people involved and how accessible things are for the young people in attendance, a quality environment is about much more than just a building. And when we're creating spaces for children, it's not just about what looks fancy to our adult eyes; it's about how it feels. If you've ever been in a kid's den, you'll know the joy that those higgledy diddley little blanket forts afford them (and us, too, if we can let go). Often in our modern age, we believe that more complicated is better and focus on how things look but simplicity often feels more nourishing.

Schools also don't have to be bound by the building walls. The kids I met during my research were part of the wider community. The whole local area was their learning environment. On one particular day, we all bundled into the school bus for an adventure to IKEA. We whizzed through the streets laughing, playing and getting rowdy listening to videogame-inspired rap music. The children spent the day running round the store and adventuring, free roaming without rules and restrictions. In that moment, IKEA was school. The learning was rich as they played and explored, discovering their place in the world and within consumer culture, too. Their free existence was also poking holes in the expectations of their social group. Other shoppers not only got to experience a deviation from the script which states that children should be kept on leashes but they also got to witness joyful, playful humans simply existing, stirring their inner child to remember how that feels.

Free iced tea bags were being given out in IKEA and the kids had come away with tonnes of them. They were counting the collective haul in the van on our way home and do you know what happened when we got back? The tea bags were equally distributed. They pooled their resources and then split them equally between every member of the group. Nobody had told them to do this and not one of them objected to it. There was this invisible, unwritten yet shared understanding. Gold is to be shared.

Space Ownership

Now, cast your mind back to your school days. Where were the important places when you imagine the map of your school? For me, it was the playground. This vast, open space that we could claim and give meaning to. We had 'kissy cats' corner'; everyone knew that was the place you went to kiss. The edge of the playground where the wall jutted out a bit and you were out of sight of the lunch staff. The classrooms themselves didn't really hold any significance as we weren't able to project our meanings and culture into the space.

This is something to really consider when we are examining spaces for education. Having neutral space is really important, but many alternative provisions take place in borrowed buildings that have already been designed and defined. As I mentioned previously, one of the schools I visited in the States took place in a church hall; the other was in an old mainstream elementary (primary) school.

The elementary school was more impressive to my adult eyes and obviously purpose-built. Entering from the carpark, there was a large outdoor area with a few benches for sitting and eating, a medium-sized fixed play equipment structure in the centre, a large sandpit and lots of open space. The school building itself was an L-shape with specific rooms occupied for different purposes, each filled with amazing equipment. There was a library with lots of books, floor seating and some computers, an incredibly well-resourced art room, and an open space for drama and performing with a small electronic music room at the back. There were other classrooms that had more age-specific resources inside, along with a staff office which backed onto a soundproofed recording 'pod' and a kitchen. It was a beautiful place filled with beautiful things. There was also a field that the school had access to for adventures into nature or aerial silk classes, and a small farm around the corner where the school founders lived.

The church didn't stand out as impressive to begin with, and it was obvious that funding was limited. The main space was a large room where the adults would generally hang out with the younger children. Creative equipment was stored in there and it had little tables, chairs and some comfy seats, along with the snack shop. There was the gaming room with a huge corner sofa, a big screen and a little space on the floor - this room was usually filled with the older kids. There was a small playroom that opened up to an outside area with some trees and a little garden. The back meeting room was empty most of the time and had a big table, surrounded by chairs with enough seats for about 10 people. There was a kitchen that I seem to remember was off limits. Immediately outside the building, there were benches alongside some fixed play equipment and a sandpit. Round the corner was a small stage which looked out onto a large, open playground. There was lots of space outside with a carpark surrounding. Though the elementary school felt to be much more fit for purpose, when I looked through the children's eyes, I saw very different things. The church setting had more meaning to the young people.

Another of my favourite moments was getting a school tour in both places from the kids. I found it fascinating that the elementary school was described through the lens of 'this is what we do here' in relation to how the space had been designed. There were specific areas for every task. And though there was a sense of pride in the description of the space, it was very different at the other school. When I was taken for a tour of the church space, the points that were highlighted had not been designed for what was being described. Two of the boys (around 11 years old) took me over to the edge of the carpark where there were some trees. A secret place, away from adult eyes. This was the 'boys' den'. There was a mattress on the floor in the little clearing between the trees. It was simple, but the way they looked at me as they told me stories of all the cheeky adventures that they'd had in that den truly showed how special it was to them. Even though the whole setting was borrowed, they had the opportunity to design and create in that little pocket and it was therefore one of the most important places to them.

This really profound thing seemed to be occurring; when I was at the elementary school, the children saw almost through adult eyes. They described the definition of the space in the way that they had been introduced to it. "This is the art room; this is the drama space..." At the church, however, it was different. They weren't describing the physical space; they were describing how their culture had manifested there because they'd been given the opportunity to make the meaning in the environment. They got to define what the space meant.

A guy called Nicholson coined the term *loose parts* which has become of the first things that people learn about with regard to playwork theory. It makes a lot of playworkers yawn, to be honest, as it's so basic, but the basic things are often the most profound. The theory of loose parts is about having things in the environment which can be used in a variety of ways. Instead of having swings and slides and 'fixed play' equipment, that immediately shout, 'THIS IS HOW YOU PLAY WITH ME' and often only offer that one opportunity, loose parts don't say anything, really. It drives me so bonkers that we seem to have one idea for what a playground looks like - swings, slide, sandpit - and you'll find that in every park the world over. Like, seriously, what is that about? Loose parts give kids the opportunity to create meaning with their imaginations and craft their own play script, which can be different every time.

I worked for a while on a play project where we filled big storage containers with scrap materials like blocks, boxes, pipes, wrapping, wheels, tyres, tubes and anything we could get our hands on, and delivered them into school playgrounds. The kids would absolutely buzz off them! The lunch staff were less impressed, though.

The Politics of Space

Adult agenda drives design. Gardens, for instance, are usually created to look pretty, yet arguably the ones that use them the most are children when they're put out in the little play pen to get their fresh air. Cities are designed with capitalist intentions and so you'll rarely find dedicated spaces in the city for kids. Children don't have the opportunity to claim or take ownership of space because space reflects politics and power dynamics. This is where Lefebvre's work comes in. Thank you to the wonderful playwork theorist Wendy Russell for bringing Lefebvre's theories to children's environments.

Henri Lefebvre was another radical sociologist, born in 1900. I love this man's mind. He looked at the mundane and unpicked it, exploring the 'why' about the simple things in life we take for granted. He was really interested in the *construction of (social) space.* As I've mentioned, sociology is about power dynamics: who has the power and why. We can often see clearly that race, gender and class influence opportunities in life, but Lefebvre was interested in how this manifests in the physical environment. He claimed that space itself was a social construction, affecting what happens and how people operate, suggesting that design had a lot of influence over people's actions, a little bit like the *hidden curriculum* mentioned earlier. Children occupy an interesting place in his theories as in most situations, they are at the bottom of the power pyramid, usually having to 'make do' with environments that weren't created with them in mind.

The elementary school was designed for education, a place for forced learning and development. The entire environment was defined with overt or subliminal instructions about what should happen in each specific area. Every room and each section of the playground had been defined purposefully and was already filled with meaning, making it really hard for young people to overlay their own intentions and desires upon it. It affected the way they perceived and therefore functioned in the space. Yet in the church, there was very little definition of what 'should' happen in each of the areas. There weren't specific zones for different activities (the gaming room was an exception to this rule); which gave rise to an interesting opportunity for the kids to take ownership of this clearly borrowed space. They shared an invisible map which spanned the whole environment, filled with meanings specific to them and their relationships with one another, because the environment nor the adults had told them 'this is what you do here'.

If we want young people to feel valued in this world, considering their experience of space is really important. Where does youth culture get to display itself? Though there may be a tokenistic play pen, public parks are usually reserved for dog 'walking' (toileting), not for kids to play and hang out. I think this is one of the reasons graffiti is so prevalent, especially in the UK. In more progressive places, there is a tolerance for graffiti if it is deemed to be 'art'. If it makes the space look more beautiful or edgy, it is welcome. But some kid scrawling 'KATIE 4 JOHN' inside a love heart or 'BEN WOS EYA Y2K' is not welcome. It's seen as crime, an attempt to deface, to insult, to damage. But maybe instead it's an attempt to try and claim some space in the face of extremely limited opportunity.

It's not necessary to have a place specifically designed for young people to enable them to take ownership. You don't have to have a blank page. But if you are an adult facilitating experiences with young people, whether that's in your own home, a classroom or a borrowed space, ensure that you haven't defined the whole environment. Make a conscious effort to create areas that mean nothing to you and I guarantee it will mean something to them.

Let's talk about privacy for a moment. Like I keep harping on about, in the current climate, there is very little opportunity for young people to have time away from others. Lucky kids might get chance to be alone if they have their own bedrooms, but many do not have this luxury. And the decline in children's opportunity to be outside and out of ear and eyeshot of adults means that childhood privacy is on the verge of extinction.

The boys' den in the church was far removed from the rest of the school. It was in the back corner of the carpark. Another place that they flagged up as an important spot on the map was a gap behind the stage. Again, a small, dark and secret space. In a previous writing, I explored dens as a representation of the womb and the desire to return to the cosy, dark comfort and connection of mum's tummy. But perhaps there is also something key about privacy. Being able to play without being seen in a place they've been able to claim, no matter how cold, damp or dirty it is, means that kids can relax and just be themselves. Most of us can agree that we behave differently when we are being watched (mirrored in those quantum realms), but my goodness, fellow big people - don't create dens on behalf of children! Gather the materials and let them know that they are there if and when they'd like to use them.

I recently walked through the area I lived in as a 19 year old student. We created so much meaning in that place. I made friendships that I believed would last a lifetime, shared the waves of one-day-weekends in living rooms which shifted from snuggle dens to dancefloors and back again, witnessed and experienced a multitude of break-ups, breakdowns, break throughs, inside jokes and cuddle puddles, shared deep vulnerability and created a plethora of joyful memories. Some of the freest, happiest, most character-developing moments of our lives happened in those houses. And then, we left. Before long, the next wave of students arrived. The posters on the walls changed, the people in the beds shifted, the music at the parties became different, yet each of these layers is somehow kept alive in the environment due to the people that experienced them. Each September, a blank slate on the same map, where self-directed action is lived usually for the first time as the majority have only recently left their family home.

When meaning isn't dictated, something beautiful happens in space. Plant definition into environments with children sparingly. Give them the opportunity to make the meaning map.

What is left when the play moves on, when the children have left is not architecture at all but more like an engine in abeyance, subservient to the action that drives it.

Paul Claydon

Permission

Permission is an important consideration when thinking about environments for children. Most places for kids are riddled with restrictions. From being banned from playing certain kinds of games to being told off for the excitement of shouting and running, there is usually a hefty rule book that must be adhered to, especially in school environments.

One of the first things I noticed in the art room at the ALC was a huge sign on the wall that said 'YES'. People drew my attention to it over and over again during my time there and it became clear that it was the foundation of the space. Anything that could be conceived of was permitted. If the kids could imagine it, the school would do whatever it took to make it happen.

A few of the kids had started making these miniature houses. Meticulously crafting tiny beds, kitchens, bathrooms and little people, too. Such fiddly work. A group of them took it a step further and decided they wanted to explore stop motion animation, so the school provided them with equipment and off they went. They taught themselves the skills through YouTube and ended up filming a stop motion animation movie, every single element of which had been created by themselves. Yes!!!

YouTube has really changed the landscape of information sharing. And I rejoice in that change! Recently, I asked the online world about some tips for caravan renovations and was directed to YouTube. I had a moment of just witnessing how profound and anarchistic it is. Anything we want to learn can now be accessed for free from other humans. And these tutorials are created because we want to help each other out. There is probably a piece present about wanting to be seen and validated but all the best offerings have a little sprinkling of narcissism. And I know there are certain videos taken down and all that jazz, but just bask in the goodness with me for a moment. What a representation of human nature and the co-creation of knowledge!

One of the mentors shared a little story with me. A while back, the kids came to him wanting to learn some astronomy. He asked them what topics they wanted to cover, expecting the basics, but they were like, "Naaaa, we know that stuff - we wanna talk about wormholes, the fabric of space/time and quantum mechanics." My people! Throughout their little course, these kids were stitching together seriously advanced knowledge of astronomy that they'd learned from YouTube and diving into the corners of reality we as a collective can't quite get our heads round. Can you imagine how boring it would be, sat in a classroom studying the solar system on the syllabus 'appropriate for your age range', when you've been down rabbit holes like quantum physics? We have to acknowledge that children now have access to information that means their understanding of a subject can be more advanced than the adults around them, including their teachers. So many reasons to update the mainstream system.

I had quite a lot come up for me when presented with that 'YES' sign in the art room. I was invited to take part in the space in the same way as everyone else. I saw the opportunity to make clothes in the textiles corner, to use a paintbrush or a spray can, to melt, to hammer, to craft, and I shrunk. Overwhelmed with options, afraid to get it wrong, unsure of where to start, I felt totally stuck. This highlights an interesting piece when it comes to the opportunities we present and how they are presented. As a researcher in that space, I was the outsider. The outsider that everyone wanted to talk to, but an outsider all the same. One of the things mentioned again and again during my interviews was about how essential it is to feel at home in a community in order to feel safe to explore. Don't hastily snap back or retract the invitations you give to kids if they don't immediately engage. If they sit at the back for a while, let them. Just keep the offer on the table and eventually, once they've sussed out the environment and feel safe, they will come out of their shell and might just take you up on your invitation. And if they don't, what an amazing opportunity for you to process some of your rejection issues!

The kids could also create bigger, more collaborative projects that they would self-direct. A group shared with me their experiences of directing and performing an entire theatre piece. They had the inspiration and with a little bit of funding they managed to do the whole thing themselves, learning so much within that experience, from building the set and managing groups of other kids to working within time frames. When ideas of pass and fail are not in the picture and instead it's about giving the kids responsibility, real, lasting learning and development takes place. It wasn't even really about the end production as it would have been in a mainstream setting; it was all about the process. They were able to fiddle and make things harmonise, figuring things out on a practical and a relational level because the adults in the space held them in an empowering way.

Nature

Modern life is becoming more and more disconnected from nature. It's very easy for us to go weeks without connecting to the natural world, especially in more urban settings, though the benefits for health, wellbeing and cognitive development in relation to fresh air and trees are well documented. Weaving in opportunities for children to interact with nature is really important and allows them to locate themselves within the wider picture of our world.

I was doing an interview with one of the mentors up on a field that they rent not far from the school. Whilst we were chatting, one group of kids were in an aerial silks class. They were climbing 10 metres up in the air on strips of silk suspended by a huge metal frame. It was beautiful to witness. Some of them were still getting to grips with holding their own body weight, whilst others had learned certain tricks and were able to spin themselves round and create little cocoons for themselves whilst they hung. Another group had been off in the woodland hunting for bugs and excitedly bounced round us upon their return, displaying the insects and lizards they'd caught temporarily in little plastic boxes. They were able to recite all manner of interesting facts and had got to know these tiny creatures through meeting them in real life, not through a textbook.

I had another life changing moment when I milked a goat. Have you ever touched a goat's teat? I can now say that I have and my skin still shivers a bit with it. It freaked me out! We were at the farm, another of the offsite parts of the school, and this little nine year old boy grabbed my hands, placing them on the teat as he demonstrated the action, laughing as I cringed my way into the process. There was a deep sense of success and celebration when I heard the milk ting into the metal bucket. The best bit though, was seeing the boy's chest swell as he taught me what to do.

Every day, the kids were invited to help with the farm chores and come rain or shine there would be a group that opted to get their wellies on and get stuck in. They loved it. It's so important for us to have opportunities to develop relationships with the non-human aspects of this world. And I don't mean in a far-out, Steiner way. Giving space for kids to have wild experiences with animals and nature is essential, not only for wellbeing but to understand where we sit in the wider reality. It's so easy for us to get lost in this grandiose illusion of humanity, elevating ourselves above the rest of the natural world that deserves our honour and respect, even if only because we recognise that we depend upon it for our survival. Gaia don't need us, but we sure need Her!

THE MENTORS

One thing almost guaranteed in alternative education settings is that the adults involved really value children. The people I've met in these spaces are there because they want to create change. Passionate activists that genuinely enjoy being around children, devoted to creating space for kids to be themselves. And in all honestly, there has to be some kind of vocation operating as the pay is usually peanuts.

I want you to think back to being a child or a teenager. Who influenced you? Who inspired you? Who had the biggest impact upon you, positively or negatively?

These influences were not usually about what people directly taught us; it was about who they were, how they behaved in the world and how they related to us. Their existence, as opposed to what they shared 'on purpose', shaped us. And this, I would say, is an important consideration when deciding what to do about school. The people involved are much more influential upon children than any pedagogy or curriculum.

One of my key influences was Miss Farris when I was seven years old. She had a nose piercing and loved Egypt. We did a big project about it and I made a pyramid, dyed with teabags. I loved sitting round listening to her stories about her experiences there. She properly **lived**, had left the pond, and not only did she have stories but you could feel it in her being. She was so cool! And so free. Miss Farris inspired us because of who she was, not because of the parts of the syllabus she taught us. I have two ankhs on my windowsill that I play through dimensions with regularly. Thanks for the seeds, Miss…

Self-Awareness & Role Modelling

The first thing that stood out during my research was that every adult involved in the schools had really got to know themselves. They understood that they had been conditioned to think and behave in certain ways and were trying their best to dismantle that. They were aware of their fears and expectations, guarding against unconsciously allowing these thoughts to project outward onto the children and control them in some way.

The beautiful thing that comes with self-awareness is an understanding of one's own self and personal boundaries. I've been tripped up by this a few times. I've been so devoted to creating the space for children to be free and flourish that I've often abandoned myself.

There was this really awesome afternoon where a group of us, mentors and older kids, were chatting about the colonisation of 'time' through the Gregorian calendar. We got really deep. And then we shifted into creating an essential list of experiences I needed to have before I left the States, from roller-skating to tater tots and cola floats. Y'know, one of those moments where the whole scope of the human experience is covered and everyone is buzzing… A younger girl came into the art room where we were hanging out and was saying out loud that she was looking for a hole punch. Nobody responded as we were engaged and it made me feel really uncomfortable. She eventually found the hole punch herself and left us to it.

I sat with that discomfort, moved through the judgement I felt in the moment and realised that what was being modelled was the same thing that Neill really wanted to drill home to people. It's not just about the children having rights, it's about all of us having the choice as to where we direct our energy. Self-awareness is about recognising our conditioned ideas about children and childhood that are often projected onto them and, it's about being able to have boundaries and value ourselves in all of our relationships, including those with kids.

There was another potent moment where one of the adults was letting a little girl climb up his body and flip over whilst holding her hands. She loved it and they were laughing and playing for a few minutes. She then tried to drag the mentor outside to play but he said no. Another beautiful reflection of autonomy and being open to 'the other' for as long as felt good. What these experiences model for young people is conscious relating. Ways to be with others that are not about one person having less power over the experience than the other. Adults weren't showing children that their needs are the most important thing in the space; they demonstrated that *everyone's* needs are equally important and invited them to find ways to work with that.

So often in my work as a therapist, I am relating with the conditioning that has arisen from being the 'good boy' or 'good girl'. Usually when we truly examine it, this is about self-abandonment. Sacrificing one's own needs or desires to please the other. It has been celebrated in our culture. Working ridiculous hours is given a badge of honour. Being smiley, happy and kind all the time gets you a certificate. We are conditioned to say yes. And this leads to really damaging relationships. We are driven to protect people from their own emotions, feeling responsible for how another person feels, and therefore unable express how we feel and what we want. We then expect the same in return, perceiving the other person's boundaries as a direct attack or rejection, as it must mean we have done something 'wrong' and are therefore worthless. For children to learn that it's safe to say no and that it's safe to be said no to creates a very different path to life and relating.

The Perspective of the Child

How children are seen is really important, too. When humans feel seen and valued, we flourish. If kids are held in high esteem, they feel it reflected in every element of the environment.

The mentors from the ALC and I gathered at the end of the day in one of the classrooms. The rain was hammering outside and we all sat round this big table as people shared their passions about young people and their rights. As per, I was concealing the electric pumping round my heart whilst listening to them talk. I'd invited them to chat to me about their perspectives of children, childhood and what they were doing in the school. This moment was probably the most enjoyable 'research' moment with adults. I love hearing people's thoughts and opinions, especially about topics that I care about. I find people fascinating and get so much from understanding how folk have landed at the conclusions they've drawn. We are all such deep beings! The conversation bounced from one passionate person to another, each of the mentors adding and enriching what had been said previously. At the core of everything shared on that rainy afternoon was the idea that children are full people with needs, desires and feelings that matter and deserve to be respected.

Often, immaturity is something we use as a criticism; to have less experience means your ideas and opinions are less valid as you 'just don't know yet'. Gosh I know that one. I've always been the youngest - in my family, in my peer groups – and condescending energy is something I have had to sit with a lot. But there is another side to having less experience. As we sat round that table, the mentors shared the gifts that those with fewer hours clocked in on the Earth plane bring.

For starters, children are the least conditioned and inhibited people on the planet. Little kids, if allowed to dress themselves will wear some seriously crazy outfits because that is what they desire in that moment. They live from the inside out! They can be bold and not give a fudge because they've not learned yet to care about other people's judgement. In the words of one of the mentors, "Children are still creatively **on**." I really loved this comment.

As I've mentioned, I genuinely believe that the block in the way of our creative expression is the fear that we will be rejected. Especially with little children, they aren't operating from a place of trying to be 'cool', and if we show up in that energy they will often call us out and force us to question the strange ways that we and our society operates. The ability that kids hold to just show up as themselves, authentically, is a real gift for us adults to be around. The sad fact of present humanity is that the more we grow, the more traumatic experiences we have, and usually the more guarded we become as a result. Children often demonstrate what uninhibited self-expression looks like and force us to question why we are all stuffed up and distorted. Instead of pushing children out of this superpower, the adults at the school received it as wisdom.

There was also the shared belief, in alignment with the unschooling value system, that humans are hardwired with an innate ability to grow and develop. Most of the mentors started as mainstream teachers. They learned the theories about how children need to be guided to learn and develop, but their own research, theoretically and practically, had debunked the old ideas they once embodied. Their experiences with kids revealed that whether or not they were pushed, the children would develop. One of the mentors put it wonderfully when they said, "All humans are constantly growing and evolving, but in childhood, the process is magnified. It's happening whether we are *teaching* them or not."

Often, I feel the biggest issues within our relationships are power struggles, frequently demonstrated by young people disengaged with mainstream education. They don't want to do the thing, but the parents or teachers believe that if they don't do the thing they won't grow and develop, and so a huge battle of wills takes hold. If there was greater trust in the innate growth and development process, perhaps we wouldn't automatically go into 'push harder' mode and kids might have less reason to push back.

I was musing the other day and had a huge revelatory moment where I saw just how innately 'clever' bambinos are. Babies are born surrounded by humans creating noise through their mouths to convey meaning. After a while, these little humans decode the sounds, understanding what is being communicated and then work out how to create sounds with their own bodies, to convey the meaning they desire to transmit. Like, WHOAH. If that isn't genius, I don't know what is! Babes really demonstrate the innate ability of humans to figure out what we need to know.

The Adult Role

In traditional school settings, you could say that adults are there to be in control, to mould and police. It would be quite easy to dismiss grown-ups at first glance in these self-directed spaces. If children are free to do their thing, then adults are just keeping an eye on them. But when you look a little deeper, you find that the adults are doing much, much more than it appears on the surface.

The role of the mentor in one sense was to hold back from stepping into the well-worn groove of 'power over children'. But mentors were also there to facilitate self-discovery, giving kids the space to find their individual path, passions and ways of living. There wasn't an expectation or desire to 'own' children's attention or minds. They wanted the kids to be in control of their own experiences and facilitated that. The approach to this was very different in each school, though.

In the Agile Learning Centre, adults were really involved in the creation of experiences. They offered numerous workshops and sessions (accessible for kids of any age) that young people could choose to attend or not. It was very cool. Like a festival, filled with exciting and diverse experiences. Most adults had some kind of mastery and their personal interests were really refined. One had been a science teacher and could take kids down scientific rabbit holes or facilitate explosive experiments in the carpark. They loved it!

The school was a playground for everyone; when the children weren't asking for support or facilitation, mentors could explore their own desires and interests. The grown-ups consciously embodied the natural creative process of picking something up for a while, delving in deeply and then moving on to something else, holding the transmission of what autonomy looks like in community and how the creative process manifests differently in individuals. This meant, however, that though awesomely rich and diverse, what was on offer at the school was more of a reflection of the adults. The children didn't have much opportunity to lead collective space.

It was really inspiring to witness all the ways grown-ups supported young people to realise their individual desires, though. Two boys of maybe 10 years old excitedly and proudly showed me a rough sketch of a cat play box alongside a fully formed, five-foot actualisation of the design made from wood and other bits. It was awesome! They'd been in charge every step of the way but were provided with the materials and tools they needed, along with guidance to develop gaps in their skillset to make it happen. This is the nuanced edge that we as adults are here to navigate if we are to support children and not take over. They don't have the cash to buy the things and might need a little bit of holding to operate certain machinery to begin with, but if we are going to empower young people, we must learn to sit on our hands when the temptation to do it for them rears its head. We might be able to do it 'better' but that *so* isn't the point. It's not about the end product; it's about the process.

The adults at this school would also teach sometimes, leading workshops and sharing their skills. If kids wanted to learn something that none of the mentors had already mastered, they would bring someone in. It was all about facilitating what the kids wanted. I love teaching and being taught, but we gotta separate the idea that teaching and force-feeding are the same thing. Consent is the key. With the coercive piece dismantled, a relationship of trust of self and of others developed. The kids felt safe to ask for help, support and guidance and could attend inspirational workshops, but they knew that they were capable as individuals and were in the operating seat of their experiences.

Offering things for kids and allowing them to choose can bring up stuff for us adults. I've had experiences where I've planned these amazing things and then nobody showed up. Oh, the sting. The rejection stories. But also, yay for triggers and being able to let go of some of our historic woundings. All the adults I met were actively practicing the art of not taking things personally, which is essential if we are to facilitate free experiences.

Each adult in the ALC had a *band*. Kids of a similar age were grouped together and had a specific mentor, a bit like a form teacher in mainstream schools. Every morning, the bands met to check in and set intentions before going off and doing their own thing. They met again at the end of the day for reflections and closing the space. This provided a feeling of holding and reminded me of an attachment model called *the circle of security*. It offers visual representation of healthy attachment through the image of a parent allowing their child to go off and explore whilst continuing to witness them with arms outstretched from afar. As the child goes off to discover the world, they feel safe as they know that they can return to their caregiver anytime. They feel reassured by the presence of their parent but are free to be in control of their own experiences for as long as they choose. I feel that the kids at the ALC felt safe to take risks because they knew they were being held. If the community feels safe, the environment can be explored.

When I first arrived at the Sudbury school, I felt a bit judgey. I'd gone from a really rich, all singing, all dancing, super stimulating environment, to a place where nothing was offered, other than the environment itself. What quickly emerged, however, was that the children's personalities, as opposed to what they were doing, were the biggest and brightest things in the space. And this comes back, as it does again and again, to the question of what our intentions are with education. Are we trying to build something in children? Or are children simply figuring themselves and their realities out in that period of their lives? Though there was seemingly less going on in the Sudbury school, the relationships and youth community were stronger. The adults stripped themselves right back and this meant the kids created the culture. The irony within this was that one of the most popular activities whilst I was visiting was actually inspired by the experiences of a mentor when they'd been a kid at a Sudbury school. Foam swords! And wow, it was so much fun. The swords were crafted with swimming noodles and duct tape that adults would help to create if asked, and then the games would commence. It was so much fun! And accessible for all members of the community. The little kids and the bigger ones would all be playing together, running round, howling and laughing, figuring out micro-conflicts and deepening their relationships.

When chatting with the school's founder, she explained how difficult it was to train the uninitiated into the 'just wait' approach. It's so easy for adults to lead, but to share one's own interests without taking charge or pushing is a very difficult edge for people to ride. The sword inspiration had come from a mentor sharing their experiences as an anecdote and the children then decided they wanted to try it for themselves. Though subtle, this is really different from one day rocking up with the equipment and making swords. It's about waiting to be invited.

As their role was less about offering or facilitating experiences, there was a richer social connection between grown-ups and kids at this school. I'd often see adults sat on their laptops or engaged in their own activities within the space, whilst having really open conversations with young people. There was an authentic and very clearly cherished friendship between them, and I saw multiple instances when the divide between adults and children disappeared. The adults were *honorary children*, accepted into their culture, and the kids were honorary adults, too.

In both the spaces I visited, mentors were their real selves and everything therefore resonated with a deep level of authenticity. One of the girls in an interview shared that mentors were, "Hired to be like an open book for kids." If relationships are conditional and hypocritical, we are setting a standard that will be carried throughout life. How can we expect kids to be real with us when we aren't real with them? Like I've said, most of us have a lot of work to do in the area of relationships and I wonder if this is because of the strange, fake relating we experience with adults in our early life.

Though I know lots of people are very protective of the Santa Claus story and believe it brings magic to children's lives, I feel that it takes more than it gives in the long run. I know this is probably gonna get me on the naughty list but like I've said, I'm a snowflake! Children get to a point where they realise that all the adults in their lives have been lying to them, and more fool them for being so immature that they didn't see through it. I remember being totally span out when I discovered the truth. It was brutal! I was one of the final ones in our class to find out and had to face the ridicule from my peers for my immaturity and then had to deal with the betrayal of trust I felt from my mum.

Not only that but the Santa story also transmits strong conditioning about being 'good' - submissive - and therefore deserving of presents. To disobey is to be 'naughty' and you receive nothing. What happens when Mum hasn't a penny to her name when Christmas rolls round? The kids learn that they've been 'bad' and aren't worthy of love in the form of gifts but actually it's because they're living in poverty. When we tell kids fairy tales and stories, there is magic and a fantasy transmission. I'm not against that. But there's something in the Christmas lie that sets up a really deep wound. I know, I'm a Scrooge. Sorry/not sorry.

CHILDREN'S CULTURE

Getting a pass into the private world of kids is my ultimate fulfilment spot. To be trusted enough for them to show their real selves and the secrets of what they get up to when adults aren't around is such a gift!

Though we have created this notion of grouping kids of the same age together through school, children give much less weight to age than adults do. I watched as a five year old, a girl of about nine, a tweenager and a mentor played cards together. The rules weren't being bent for anyone but there were different dynamics playing out, almost like a little family. The little one was snuggled into the mentor, the nine year old was sat alone and concentrating meticulously and the tween was sarcastically narrating the whole experience. Each of them brought a different energy to the group and it created such a rich scene. Because the school itself wasn't plugged into age hierarchy, there wasn't a desire to disregard younger children as they weren't 'cool enough' or a glorification of the older ones either, creating a much more relaxed and genuine mesh of relating.

There were clusters of age groups at other times but the way they all shared the space was profound to witness. The teenagers would be hanging out talking about things they'd seen on the internet on couches, whilst little kids made a den under the table. The space was shared, all representations of childhood culture were welcome and there was harmony within the anarchy of the space. In another moment, two boys were sat at a desk with a full-size electronic keyboard hooked up to a computer. The older kid must have been about 12 and was sat creating a song through recording multiple piano rifts and overlaying them, skills he'd taught himself through YouTube. The younger kid was only about five and was also able to play the same technical rifts, but every time he touched the piano he was told, "Please stop." And I mean, the older kid was deep in his creative process, so it made sense that he didn't want someone else faffing with the keyboard at the same time. The thing I found interesting, though, was the lack of aggression. The younger kid wasn't told to go away, and though it didn't feel exactly comfortable or harmonious, they shared the space and that moment together as two equal people.

Adulteration is a term from playwork theory which is basically about the ways kids are conditioned out of being themselves and end up becoming mini adults. Often simply an adult being present in a space can adulterate an experience; the kids will respond differently, changing their behaviour or opinions in response. Who knows how that keyboard dynamic would have played out if I wasn't there. But it's not just about kids 'behaving' - it's also about trying to be grown up to gain more respect. They will often appear to be mature for their age, but it isn't always authentic.

Sometimes the children raised in more progressive environments end up spending most of their time with adults and it changes them. I saw this very clearly within a few of the interviews in my research. In one particular session, I was chatting to a couple of girls who were on the brink of their teenage-hood. They proudly reflected back some of the arguments for self-directed learning I'd heard from parents and mentors, and I could feel all the ways they wanted to impress me. I'm not judging them for that, but it felt like instead of sharing what it was like to be **in** the experience, they were regurgitating what they'd heard from the surrounding adults. Even if we are really passionate about children's rights, their heads don't need to know the ideology to enable their participation to be actualised. Sometimes filling kids up with ideas can have an almost opposite effect.

It's really key for adults to let children have the time and space to develop their own ideas by stepping back. They often want adults around, especially cool adults! But we still hold a ridiculous amount of influence over them, whether that is because they fear us or really respect us. They are being conditioned all the time through their experiences, so having the space to figure out and establish their own culture away from adult influence is really important. I can almost guarantee that the most treasured memories you and I have from childhood don't have adults in them.

Risk

Now more than ever, it's incredibly important to weave opportunities for risky play into the spaces children inhabit. Though breaking bones and having accidents was pretty grim when I was a kid, it was also a rite of passage. And I mean getting a fluorescent pot that all your mates could tag was so cool! Jabbing knitting needles down said pot when the itch took hold was less pleasant, but there was so much learning and initiation that came through those accidents.

We live in a seriously risk adverse society (another awesome book to read is Tim Gill's *'No Fear'*) but news flash, folks - health and safety isn't about eliminating risk, it is about having a plan for what happens if stuff goes wrong. We've got it twisted in most places, especially with children, thinking that the responsible thing to do is to wrap them up in cotton wool and keep them safe. But we are robbing them of essential learning and fun experiences when we do that.

A little girl was tracing a picture from the computer of a character from a cartoon. She'd made all these rad little toys through drawing on bigger pieces of plastic and then shrinking them down using a heat gun. The girl chuckled whilst recounting the number of times she'd burned herself, explaining why she now asked for help with the heat gun from a mentor. Her creations were really cool and I could see the skill she had developed through all that blistery, trial and error and the process had been empowering, she was given the opportunity to try on her own and then decided that she needed support. The mentor supporting her had been a gymnast as a kid and broke her neck in practice. Once she was out of the hospital, she was back in the gym doing the same trick that led to her injury. "And that," she shared, "is my philosophy. There will be burns and mess but from there, there will be learning, skills development and a sense of pride and success."

It's important to realise that most kids will approach new things with caution. It's rare to find a young person that puts themselves in danger. Kids are more switched on that we give them credit for. They surprisingly don't want to get hurt and will often seek guidance and support to figure things out, and the more they get chance to assess their own risk, the more that ability develops within them.

I did have an edgy moment, though. Y'see, this dynamic of power between adults and kids, and sometimes between children themselves, can stimulate this desire to 'show off' and perhaps not risk assess as they are performing. Following a lot of excitement during a foam sword battle, this one kid climbed up onto the roof with one shoe on as I watched from the ground with the other kids. I could see that he was messing around and being a bit silly, and what I knew about the adult presence sometimes pushing kids past their boundaries was ringing in my brain. I could feel he was on the edge and so I took a deep breath and walked away. The girls rallied round to help him down and all was well. But this is another reason that kids need space. As we are automatically seen as authority figures, some kids respond to that by fluffing themselves up and pushing to demonstrate how able they are, losing the connection to themselves and their instincts in the process.

Gaming

Computer games don't affect kids. I mean, if Pac-Man affected us as kids, we'd all be running around in darkened rooms, munching magic pills and listening to repetitive music.
Anon

(Fun Fact - For many years as a kid I thought 'Anon' was the name of a famous writer.)

One of the absolute highlights of my time with the young people I met was playing video games. *'Super Smash Bros.'* was released in 1999 and featured strongly in my own gaming days; I had no idea it was still going but as we all sat snuggled in the gaming room, I was secretly experiencing eye-watery waves of nostalgia. I've always had big performance anxiety but there's a feeling of protection I get when playing a character on a game, so when they invited me to play, I said yes. I was with the older guys (around 11 years old) and five of us were sat, controllers in hand, choosing the character that would either make or break us in the fight. The gang were eager to help me out and showed me the ropes. My excuse for getting rinsed every round was that I didn't know the controls anymore (we weren't playing on a Nintendo 64 like I was back in the day), but the truth is that I've always sucked at computer games.

Something mega special happens with multiplayer gaming; everyone is super-engaged; the energy is electric and you almost enter another realm. You're in this virtual world together with rules that everyone is bound by, that cannot be manipulated. And the rules make sense, unlike the world outside. Gaming offers the perfect balance of strategy and luck. Nobody has to enforce anything; the computer does that. It is fair. It is reliable. And even when it all goes Pete Tong, you can try again next round.

It was really humbling and fascinating to witness the ways in which the young people organised who, what and how the gaming took place. This is something we often overlook when we think about the capabilities for self-organisation that children possess. Us adults love to feel that we are required to make things harmonious. But the reality is that we aren't. I sat there watching as games were suggested to play next and they decided together how many rounds before they passed the controller on. Other young people came in and out of the room. There was a bookings schedule on the wall with half hour slots; you put your name down to reserve your turn but could jump in if nobody had booked on.

There was one point where some of the younger kids wanted to play (five years old) and though the older ones rolled their eyes, knowing they wouldn't have the challenge that they would like from someone that had equal skills in the game, they let them play. Everyone that wanted one had a turn. The younger kids hadn't booked on but space was made for them. There was such a deep and embodied sense of 'rightness' that hadn't been drilled in through an adult, or a reward and punishment scheme. And though these were competitive games, there was no sense of competition inflicted in the structure of the school, and so the winning or the losing had no weight within the social dynamics of the group. The room was full all the time, some people playing and others watching, beside kids sat on their own devices in their own worlds.

A lot is said about video games for young people, often by people who have never actually played them. And I get it - it is a relatively new phenomenon and when people don't understand things, they are afraid of them. But gaming offers a place in the world and a culture for people that don't fit into popular culture. And this has expanded exponentially since I was involved. I remember when online gaming became a thing, I spent many a night with my first boyfriend and his best friend, smoking a ridiculous amount of weed and watching them play *'Halo'* or *'Call of Duty'* with people all over the world. The guys didn't have a big group of friends around them, they didn't want to go to the pub or go clubbing; they wanted to get high and game. And the friendships that they cultivated and shared with these people were deep! Back in my childhood, before the days of the internet, if you were a loner and didn't fit in, you didn't have friends. But that isn't the case anymore. Gaming offers an interactive world where you can meet other weirdos and realise that you *do* fit in, you have a place and you have people, too.

One of the things often thrown at video games is that they're violent. I have known and grew up with a lot of violent lads. And I've worked with many, too. Do you know what's funny, though? None of them were gamers. The 'Am well 'ard and am gonna batter you' young people are usually beating up the kids that play video games, no matter how violent the games are. My experiences in life, especially as a therapist, suggest that violence is stimulated by intense emotions and reactivity – it's more about what's going on inside than just mimicking what has been seen. Don't get me wrong; witnessing domestic violence or being beaten up can encourage some people to re-enact these experiences in their relationships, but I don't feel that playing a violent video game has the same effect.

Researching for this book has been such a rollercoaster; sometimes the things I read filled my body with the amazing feels of YES, while at other times, it has made my skin crawl. The beauty of writing non-academically is that I get to be me and don't have to cover up my non-neutrality about what I'm sharing with you. *Nurturing Young Minds,* (2017) is a collection of writings by Australian researchers and writers edited by Dr Ramesh Manocha. It has quite a few chapters dedicated to the risks of technology, internet usage and gaming for young people. Though there were some key and interesting points made, there were also others that brushed me up the wrong way.

Though I don't like to admit it, there is research which links violent video game usage to hostile thoughts and feelings for teenagers. Our good friend The Media managed to convince us that the horrific instances involving school shooters, where students have tragically massacred classmates and teachers with guns, are related to violent computer games. I'm not saying that the two things are not correlated, but there are so many more factors at play here. Like public access to firearms (passing swiftly by that rabbit hole), experiences at home, trauma, mental health... And what about the mainstream news? At any time throughout the day, the horrors of what humanity is doing to itself is publicly and graphically broadcasted to anyone with a TV, regardless of their age. And this stuff is real. It's not fiction. It's not a scary film or show: it is real life. Surely what we doing as a collective influences young people more than a violent game?

Another piece brought to the table by *'Nurturing Young Minds'* was about physical exercise and becoming sedentary. This I can really see. When joy and community come through a virtual world, getting out into the trees and using our own bodies is less appealing, and this has a negative impact on our physical, mental and emotional health. I've seen many gamers slowly turning a bit grey. Research also demonstrates that excessive gaming causes bad posture and though fine motor skills (like using fingers and hands) go up, there is a definite decline in gross motor skills (like walking and physical co-ordination).

Did you know there is actually a disorder called 'Problematic Internet Use'? Oh, how we love a label in this modern day! From what I can gather, this was brought forward by Kim Young in the mid-90s. It's probably lost its stick now, as a disorder that we all embody just doesn't pack the same punch. There's also *Internet Gaming Disorder* and there exists a heap of professionals waiting to diagnose and treat your gamer child for their illness. But again, gaming, if out of balance and done excessively, is a symptom of something deeper going on, like any kind of excessive escapism. And really, what we are talking about here is addiction.

I feel there are two sides of addiction. There are certain substances that our brains can get hooked on but there are also aspects of our personality or reality that we want to escape, arguably as a result of traumatic experience. Self-directed communities and schools can often be operating from a space of fierce dedication to self-regulation, which I fully support. Yet there is another piece here that must be recognised. If we look closely, we as a global society are seemingly, hopelessly addicted to both screens and sugar. I'm not going into the why of that right now, but I do feel that there is a certain responsibility for boundaried interaction with these things. This might contradict the notion of self-direction for young people, but surely we wouldn't get a kilo of smack (heroin), pop it on the table and let kids decide if they want to take it? Everything is always contextual. And one of the things I've noticed is that often screen time and sugar intake is approached with strict adherence to the self-directed philosophy. But both are really addictive. Do we really want to create self-directed addicts?

I have met a lot of unschoolers who put no limitation on sugar and screens, the reasoning behind which is about children being in control of themselves and learning to self-regulate. There is often this idea of, 'We give it power if we put boundaries around it' but the reality is that addictive substances have power. Chemically. I recently saw a post from an unschooler sharing that their child had just been diagnosed with diabetes, which sadly didn't shock me.

As a playworker, you are trained to be really present and in tune with your triggers, examining the 'why' of your reactions before you take any action. If it's about personal baggage, you're trained to pop it to the side so that you can show up from a clear space with the young people you're working with. In a play setting, the rules are a bit different, but in life, what are our responsibilities for the kids in our care? Are we resisting putting any limitation on young people's usage because we are also addicts?

One of the schools I visited didn't have video games on offer. They kept it out of the setting all together, which to me feels like a real shame. There were computers, all lined up in a row and young people were given a very minimal amount of time to play on them. But there was no collective play. They also had quite strict restrictions about what could be brought to the school for lunch. Sugar wasn't permitted. Yet at the other school, there were no restrictions around sugar or screens. I consumed a lot of sugar when I was a kid and my relationship with it even now is an uphill battle. Part of me resents it being so accessible when I was a child. The argument is often that if sugar was introduced now, it would be a class A drug.

During my research, I noticed that there were two varieties of parents allowing self-direction: the ones that weren't quite sure and needed a lot of support to let go of their fears, and then the ones who had totally let go and were unsure of when and if they were ever meant to step in with their children. For me, it is all about boundaries. Children do have vulnerabilities due to their age that we need to protect. Neill spoke a lot about the boundaries between adults and children to respect each person's freedom, I feel there is more to it now, perhaps because of where we are at in the world with consumerism.

The world in the 60s was a very different version of the world which exists today. Following two world wars that plunged the majority into poverty, there has been an explosion which feels to be crescendoing in the present time. In the west, not only do we have access to things but that access is unlimited. We have enough money to eat what we want when we want. And the toxic stuff is really appealing as it's so addictive. We have screens which we carry round in our pockets and can use at any moment. As adults, we might have developed the awareness that we need to create a little bit of space between ourselves and these electronic devices, or that our relationship with sugar or junk food is making us ill and therefore we need to make a change, but children often have not developed this capacity yet.

One of the things I find incredibly important individually is integrity. I won't sit a course with or listen to the advice of someone who isn't embodying what they are teaching. It drives me mad. And I see it all the time with children and adults. 'Do as I say, not as I do.' It's no wonder that teenagers reject the restrictions placed upon them when they see caregivers living very differently, Mum is putting all the boundaries around screens for the young people in the family but she is on her phone all the time. Perhaps there is a shift that can be made together? I would love to see greater levels of authentic communication in the adult/child relationship; maybe we grown-ups can share our own struggles with these addictive pieces of modern life and commit to having the same boundaries around them as the young people in our care.

Gender and Sexuality

Men and women, Adam and Eve; these binary ideas of who people *should* be due to the sex they were born with are ever so restrictive. Just like childhood, *gender* is argued to be a social construction. We have been taught so many things about what it means to be a man or a woman. Luckily, these themes are being deconstructed by the good old snowflakes, building upon the work of some very wonderful pioneering activists and theorists.

The deconstruction arguably first began with Feminism, because the cut between man and woman resulted in women not being afforded the same opportunities in the world. Historically, systematically anyone that wasn't a white man was(/is) seen as less than and subordinate to them. Though the Suffragettes lost their lives so that women could vote, the inferior position of 'housewife' remained firmly intact until the second wave of Feminism in the late 1960s. And in certain cultures, it hasn't moved on.

Recently I walked out of the gym and got chatting to a Pakistani woman. I go to a women's only gym and about 99% of the women there follow Islam. We started chatting as she is a high school teacher and as she got close to the car she was laughing, saying that the white women at school didn't know how good they had it. Though she worked full time now, her responsibilities at home hadn't diminished. She was still responsible for cooking all the meals and doing the housework, so from the gym, after a full day teaching, she was heading home to make dinner for her family and put a wash on. The struggle still very much exists in different ways for different social groups. The notions and ideas of women as a subordinate group of people are still very much rooted in our world.

I remember being 11 or 12 years old, beginning to roll my school skirt up and shave my legs. I wore thick orange foundation and heavy eyeliner. Puberty for me, like many, included an awakening about becoming sexually desirable. And that then meant that random men would slow down their cars and beep their horns at me. I wasn't dressing for those men; I wanted the lads I found fit at school who were 13 years old to want me, not a 50+ year old stranger. But it created this weird dichotomy within that silently exists in all women, feeling repulsed by that unwarranted desire and very unsafe because of it, whilst also desiring and feeling validated by it.

As I grew, I had numerous conditionings contradicting within me and limiting my experiences. I was taught to 'want' sex and that saying no isn't what good or sexually appealing girls do, so I found myself having numerous sexual experiences that I didn't want. I saw the ways that I would be listened to if men were attracted to me, how there was this magnetic force that ran through sexual desire that I could harness, but how more often than not I didn't feel safe in my body and therefore couldn't take up space. I witnessed the housewife life of my grandmother and saw the ways in which my grandfather doubted my abilities to be self-employed and successful - ideas he didn't have about my self-employed, male cousin of the same age. I saw after parties dominated by the guys as the women faded into the background until it was home time/hook up time. I felt it all.

Until I read Feminist texts, I couldn't contextualise my experience. And this is the way with privilege. It's invisible until it's not, and then you see it everywhere. Feminism really helped me to understand social conditioning and the ways systems are built around these ideas. It helped me to recognise that conditioning becomes embodied within us all and normalised. It lit a fire within me to expel those ideas from my being. It helped me to understand that people see 'woman' as lots of differing things and trying to fit into them all was hurting and restricting me. I continue to strip the layers of what it means to be 'woman' from my mind and attempt to do the same for my body.

I know that men have lots of expectations and ideas planted within their minds and bodies too. The difference is that the modern world has been built by white men with their conditionings, which means it's easier and more validating for people that fit that description to navigate it. The expectations for men and women are different and so are the permissions. That said, what once afforded some kind of acceptance and ease is now in other ways a reason for heavy judgement and damnation. The current collective awakening which is unshackling the world must be really bloody hard to consciously navigate as a white man. But I know incredible beings doing just that. Bless us all and the clean-up mission of this time on the planet. So many layers of trauma and conditioning that we're softening to see, feel and release.

I was recently involved in a community project where unconsciously the group that had been brought together for the board were all white and I was the only female. This is a prime example of how this stuff continues to manifest when we're not aware of it and making different choices accordingly. If we choose not to see or delve into actively dismantling, the systematic conditionings continuously replicate through us. 'We're all one' is a sweet gesture but we've all got unconscious bias that continue the codes of oppression. It's therefore really important for us to be doing 'the work' and for these understandings to be held in our awareness as we create spaces for children.

In 1990, Judith Butler, a Feminist theorist and professor, published the book '*Gender Trouble*' which, for the first time really, opened the conversation questioning what gender actually is. She introduced the idea that gender is performed in response to conditioning. My essence feels like a woman, so therefore I will subconsciously perform that role. But what happens when our essence doesn't match up with the expectations of our biological sex?

Social life has been built upon conditioned *heteronormativity* - everyone is straight, people with penises are men embodying all the ideas that we have around what makes a *man,* and people with wombs are women embodying all the ideas that we have around what makes a *woman*. It's argued that this is natural and anything out of that natural order is an illness. Women are sweet and soft; men are strong and bold. And our unconscious bias means we interact with ourselves and one another accordingly, with weird expectations to boot. We have made impressive progress, especially within the realm of sexuality as a collective. There is more permission than ever before for us to love who we want to love. But gender conditioning starts young and we're still working through these themes.

Before a child is born, one of the first questions we ask is about their gender and the way that we perceive them is set up from that moment. You and I may have different ideas about the life path and identity for a boy or a girl, but we do expect different things from each. I for one am over the moon that we're collectively beginning to question these things. We are trapping our children into suffocating boxes, and this is why the 'snowflakes' or 'rainbows' or radical children of the now, are saying, "NA, MATE! I'm gonna deconstruct your box and throw it back at you." If gender is a collection of performed stories and expectations, does it exist when we are genuinely being ourselves?

If we are to embody this notion of self-direction to the core, that also means within our identity, too. I read a wonderful book recently called *'Trans Power'* (2019) by Juno Roche. For them, their *trans* label has been an ultimately liberating identity to adopt, as they say there is no 'right way' to perform it. It is a hybrid form, free of expectation. Their body, born with a penis, has now been crafted into what they call a 'cave'. They don't define themselves as a *man* or a *woman* but something totally new, self-created and in-between.

> *Trans is empowerment and autonomy, inhabiting my frame and my frames of reference... Trans represents freedom for me, not just a place to stay put in a borrowed surface or on borrowed time.*
>
> Juno Roche

The book was so powerful, another one I sobbed reading. One of the main things I took from it was about the two sides of being *queer*. The liberation from expectation and a fierce reclaiming of individual identity outside of patriarchal, binary notions, yet also a deep loneliness that comes from not belonging within these sick patriarchal ideas. It's a flipping brave path to be trans or queer. Many people still don't get it and violently oppose it. We're so stuck in duality throughout all layers of our being and reality.

One of the arguments brought forth in the book referenced how trans women are not *real women* and this really made me think. What actually makes a woman? Is a woman who has had a hysterectomy a real woman? What about someone who has had lip fillers and breast implants? Is a *real woman* covered in body hair or clean shaven?

Our bodies and our identities are innately individual. Our sexual desires, our pleasure, our flesh - we have to learn about these things ourselves through exploration. Our bodies are our own Earths and have their own maps that we must discover and explore independently. That said, the social group of 'women' has faced terrible oppression that still exists systemically and we must navigate all of that, too. From what I can gather, the way out of this is about 'queering the norm'. And I saw some wonderful manifestations of this during my research.

Queering the Norm

Self-directed and autonomous spaces give rise to ultimate individuality, attracting people that live from that same space. Over half of the adults in one of the settings I visited were queer. There was no formalised teaching about gender identity or sexuality but the space was open for those conversations if they arose. And people, regardless of age, were called out when being unconsciously inappropriate and invited to explore topics, explicitly or implicitly. The adults were a living transmission that existed outside of heteronormativity. "Here I am, a whole person, that contradicts expectation and cannot be crammed into a box." Funky haircuts and appearances, fluid gender identity, tattoos and freedom were so embodied that it naturally inspired and permitted the young people in the space, too. The message was loud and clear: 'Your identity, however it wants to be expressed right now, is welcome and honoured, and so is mine.'

My sexual orientation is difficult to define. Though I lean more toward men, I have had relationships with women; and I'm attracted to personal qualities as opposed to a specific gender. This has and still causes me confusion in a world that wants me to define myself, and also causes difficulties in communicating with the world who I am open to and what I'm available for. These binary boxes make it difficult for our identities to be claimed and expressed. I used to think it was important to have adults that young people felt were just like them, but what feels important now is to have role models that are completely themselves. Though they may be very different from the young people, having adults that fly their freak flags means that there is a deep permission for everyone else to do the same.

I remember one little bean in particular, as he clambered onto my lap with his red and gold flared trousers dangling from my knees, the millimetre of hair on his seven year old head brushing upon my chin as he happily rolled Fimo on the table in front of us. His painted pink fingernails sliced the Playdough with a Stanley blade into little chunks as he told me all about his love for Diana Ross. I had to conceal tears of joy once again in this instance. He was so comfortable and felt safe to present himself, internally and externally, in the way which felt good and in integrity to him in that moment. And him being trusted with a Stanley blade was the icing on the cake!

The key within all of this, though, is to let everything remain fluid in our responses and expectations, forever. To queer the norm is to give permission every single step of the way. Though I'm lucky enough to feel connected to femininity and not to have had the deeply challenging experience of feeling disconnected from or trapped by my biological sex, I present differently every single day. Some days I wear heels and skirts and makeup, other days I'm in fat skate trainers, a hoody and baggy pants. Some days I feel soft and quiet and introverted, other days I feel sociable and giddy and bold. We must permit one another to be ourselves. And our 'self' is not fixed. Not one bit.

A few years ago, I was working with an awesome 10 year old, formally diagnosed as being on the Autistic Spectrum. To me, he was simply a super cool human that I would go on adventures and play 'Pokémon Go' with. Up until this point, the gender debate hadn't really come into mainstream discussions, but I'd grown up partying with some incredibly creative people, some of whom were very fluid within expressions of their gender and sexuality. I hadn't really been exposed to people who felt confused about their gender identity, though - it didn't need to be defined in our community. And on a personal level, it's hard to imagine what that experience would feel like as I've not felt it.

This one day, me and my 'Pokémon Go' friend were walking past a fancy-dress shop; he was really disappointed that it was shut because he wanted "to try on girls' dresses". It turned out his dad was very fixed in his ideas of what a little boy should be and how they should dress and play, not because he was bad or stupid but because of his own conditioning. At the time, I was living with a beautiful gay man who was launching a gender fluid clothing range which included some funky skirts. After speaking to Pokémon's mum, I invited them to my house for a day of dressing up and fun; it is still one of those memories that makes my eyes leak and hairs stand up on end. There he was, in the clothes he really wanted to wear in that moment, living his best life, glancing over at his mum like, "Am I really allowed to do (and be) this?" And there she was, with a heart filled with pride and permission, saying a big fat "YES".

Especially within spirituality focused progressive communities, I've noticed quite archaic notions of what men and women 'should' be, argued to be based upon nature. Heck, a lot of people believe that gender fluidity is a conspiracy to mess up humanity! It always feels so ironic to me that if we are leaning closer to the conditioning around what we should look like in relation to our biological sex, we celebrate it but when people are adapting their bodies toward the opposite gender people have such toxic reactions.

What we are really talking about here is identity and a desire to express ourselves freely. The expression of our ever-changing deepest selves, on the outside. If an environment facilitates freedom of expression for children, we are at least half the way there. Let's leave the boxes outside and welcome young people to express themselves as they desire, recognising that if their identity triggers us, it is our responsibility to heal and nothing to do with them.

Sex

The sex taboo is the root evil in the suppression of children.

A. S. Neill

Our mate Neill from Summerhill extended the idea of autonomy throughout all aspects of life, even sexuality. He lived through the sexual revolution and you can feel its influence upon his writings. Despite this revolution, in the current times we are still journeying through sexual repression, especially in the UK. Sexual pleasure is taboo and cast out as wrong from the moment it begins. I mean, how many of us as children were allowed to experience desire and explore our own bodies? It's not generally permitted or acceptable; in fact, it is usually shamed, which is most probably why our sexuality gets pushed into dark, hidden corners of our lives. When we really strip it down though, isn't it crazy? Our bodies are these incredibly sensitive instruments able to experience immense levels of pleasure, yet we deny ourselves and our children the permission to explore and experience. When we are disconnected from our bodies, all manner of distortions develop to help us cope.

Neill shared that most children that ended up at Summerhill had already begun to embody a *diseased attitude* toward sex and sexuality. At his time, the 'wrongness' of sexuality was explicit - Catholicism taught that sex was sinful and the majority were indoctrinated. Though many of us now can brush off these ideas as untruths, they are still held in our bodies. We carry this shame, robbed of the opportunity to get to know our sexual selves with a heap of unfulfilled desires that we feel wrong for having. I would say this is why the porn industry thrives so much; watching others and having fantasies in secret because we don't feel safe to experience things ourselves in loving and consensual spaces with others. We're so scared of being rejected or seen as 'wrong' for our desires that we have to watch other people instead.

During my studies, Jacky Kilvington and Ali Wood (two very special playworkers) published a book called, '*Gender, Sex and Children's Play*' (2016). In it they explore numerous facets of play and sexuality, and in a similar way to Neill, call for us to release the taboos and normalise children's sexuality. In my own work as a therapist, I was the safe receiver of my clients' biggest secrets, and you'd be surprised how many of those confessions were about sexual relations with siblings during childhood. Newsflash, folks: as much as it might freak you out, it's actually totally normal.

Children play with sexuality to explore their own bodies, the difference between male and female bodies, pleasure, power, closeness - the list goes on. It's healthy. And when it isn't shamed, Neill suggests that it allows a person to carry that healthy sexuality into adulthood.

In our modern times, there is much talk of and resistance to the sexualisation of children. Pop star role models harnessing the power of sex appeal with lyrics that are 'not appropriate' for young people, for example. I grew up with the Spice Girls and distinctly remember singing '2 Become 1' on karaoke when I was about seven years old. I had no idea what the lyrics I'd memorised were about until the background of the karaoke screen was showing two people getting it on. And my family were not sex positive. We didn't talk about it. There was no frame of reference. Again, we see this thing about children's rights being about protection over permission and empowerment. What if we were as eager to provide children with the right for healthy exploration of their own sexuality instead of just protecting them from sex 'too early'? I'm not suggesting we push children's sexuality but I'm eager for us to give them space and tools to navigate their feelings and experiences, being a safe place that they can come to for support and processing. We are way off in the extreme 'sexuality is bad' end of the spectrum with kids at the moment.

There is an important thing to note about patriarchal manifestations and women's bodies being utilised to sell. Heck, I've unconsciously resorted to it within my work. Put a sexy selfie on your advertising and you're guaranteed to receive more interest. We are still breaking down using the female body as a commodity and discussions around sexuality cannot be separated from Feminism.

Don't get me wrong, there are many progressions within collective attitudes toward sex and sexuality. But the majority of 'sex education' classes are still delivered by unliberated adults that feel insanely uncomfortable discussing the topic with young people. And then there's the content. Sex anatomy is generally all that is delivered, but again, I ask you - what about pleasure? What about power relations and communication? The suppression of sexuality means that porn is often the teacher for young people. I remember my experiences as a teenager (dial up internet had just about got going by then); everyone was simply performing what we'd seen. It wasn't about feeling good. It wasn't about connecting with each other. There wasn't any kind of conversation before or after. It was just 'doing it' because you didn't want to be one of the people that wasn't. And to be honest, the whole thing was about the guy climaxing. That's what the process was leading to, and when that happened, usually very quickly, the show was over.

There was a controversial documentary a while ago called *'Sex in Class',* where a sex education program was delivered in a mainstream UK school in Accrington. It aimed to counteract the trend where teens learn about sexuality from the distortions of the porn industry and instead directly educate them about all facets of sexuality. Though the teens giggled and cringed their way through it, they were taught about exploring their own bodies, creating pleasure for themselves and one another, communicating their desires and having consensual, enjoyable, sexual experiences.

Neill believed that if the environment was sex positive, sex would be learned through discovery and exploration. And with the core of his approach being 'freedom without license', successful communication and boundary navigation was something the young people in his school were well-versed in. Throughout his writing, he refers a lot to the 'self-regulated' child, naturally developing when autonomy remains intact. They know what they want to do and do it, they know when they don't want or like something and they can stop it. This lends itself so beautifully to healthy sexuality. When authentic living is embodied from childhood, so many of the distortions we witness are dismantled. Children don't have to be taught but given the space to explore. If young people at Summerhill crossed sexual boundaries without consent, they were excluded from the school. Though Neill's ideas were and are sexually liberating, any kind of experience which lacked consent was not tolerated. This is the beauty of the way his idea's manifested. Liberation coupled with some soft and some very firm boundaries. Free unto self with respect for the other. And open communication throughout it all.

There's something about initiation missing in our modern culture. Way, way back in the day, young people would go through a ceremony to mark the transition of puberty. Instead of telling young people about what they should and shouldn't do, perhaps we can make space for vulnerability and share our own experiences when they decide that they want to know. Instead of pinning them down in their bedrooms and having 'the talk,' can we not just be open from the word go and allow them to be exposed to sexuality as a wonderful part of life? I mean, the end goal here is about growing happy, healthy humans. Instead of pretending sexuality isn't a thing until they reach teen years, forcing them to explore and 'understand' through really twisted images and videos on the internet and then having awkward conversations that make everyone want to throw up, we can do it differently.

During my research, I witnessed lots of open conversations, often stimulated by the young people themselves. And for me, that is the key to all of this. Not being afraid of sexuality, but also not pushing things either. Existing authentically. Creating spaces that feel safe for conversations. Respecting that young people might not want to tell us everything and releasing the idea that they have a duty to let us in. The internet exists. They will watch porn. So, let's be more open about what healthy sexuality looks like.

Like I mentioned when talking about adulteration, we have to bear in mind that children's oppression makes them desire to leave the realm of childhood as soon as possible. They want to grow up quickly as they believe, quite rightly, that more freedom exists when they are adults. It could be argued that chatting about sex openly might make them want to rush into it, but I feel that the pressure already exists. Young people will explore their sexuality; what is lacking in present culture are healthy expressions and examples for them to be guided by.

Race

Having role models that reflect and represent who we are is something that helps us to figure ourselves out. A good friend of mine that also exists in the 'conscious' spiritual communities of the UK has often shared with me the challenges presented through her dual heritage and the lack of representation she experiences in group spaces. The music, the faces; none of it feels to represent who she is which leaves her with a bitter taste of *otherness*. I read a post the other day on social media about a little boy with dark skin being over the moon to witness a mixed-race character in a Disney movie. This shouldn't have been a remarkable experience.

I was recently really taken aback when speaking to a dear sister of mine, who is a black woman, to discover that when George Floyd was murdered by a police officer in 2020 and the Black Lives Matter movement came into focus, not one of her white friends, including me, reached out to her. We absolutely failed her. I didn't know what to do when it all went down. I felt ashamed of my whiteness. Uncomfortable that I was allied with the oppressor because of my race. And so, I hid. I don't know what everyone else was feeling and doing but I feel that often we just stick our heads in the sand if it feels uncomfortable and doesn't directly affect us. What I'm learning more and more is that we need to lean into the discomfort. Be part of conversations. Be open to being questioned and called out. Hear what it's like to be on the other side. Allow ourselves to be used as a part of the healing process. No more hiding. Lots more listening. Softening and receiving. Holding and being guided by the ones that are hurting. Making different and more informed choices accordingly.

The children I met at the schools were nearly all white, middle class and able-bodied, which was disappointing and very revealing about where we are at. I can't really put self-directed learning into context with race as I didn't see how it manifested. I hoped that these revolutionary spaces would offer a potential remedy to class, race and ability inequality and maybe they can be as the schools operate from radical narratives based upon mutual aid. The world outside, however, does not operate through those parameters and so minority groups have additional social barriers when it comes to accessing such a school.

I feel like we have a duty to initiate young people into real history and social inequality. If not, we run the risk of creating more notions of 'we are all one, we are all the same', which though true on one level, is not reflected in the construct of society. We must get to grips with the fact that the world is harder to navigate if you're not white, middle-class, straight, cis and able-bodied. We all have our challenges but the more social groups you belong to that exist outside of the dominant group, the more challenges you have. Privilege is about what you don't have to go through.

Diversity in schools is not simply about fulfilling quotas; it is about representation. Representation for the kids and representation of all within the culture we are creating. Our experiences with the world unfold differently. Our experience is not **the** experience. And kids need to get that. If we aren't going offer a direct teaching experience about inequality and privilege, we must make sure the transmission reaches them somehow. If we want to create inclusive spaces, we need grown-ups that represent the diversity of humanity, not just for the kids to see themselves reflected back but also for them to understand what people that aren't like them have to go through. To allow the potency of those voices and experiences to be a fundamental part of culture for us all to learn from and through.

NEURODIVERSITY

I'm conflicted about labelling children. Diagnosis can support young people to access additional help and support which is often crucial to enable them to pass through institutions and get the grades they deserve. I know friends who have been diagnosed with things like ADHD later in life and it has been revelatory. They've stopped punishing themselves and believing they are broken or inept, instead understanding that they are neurologically different. That said, hearing my little Pokémon friend refer to himself judgementally as an 'aspie' broke my heart. These labels can become self-fulfilling prophesies and give children a feeling of *otherness* that is very difficult to break through.

In one of his ground-breaking and now insanely popular TED talks, Sir Ken Robinson shared the story of a little girl who simply couldn't sit still in class. He highlighted that in this day and age she would have been labelled and probably sedated, yet at the time, she was invited into the dance hall. She later became one of the most successful ballet dancers of all time.

ADHD

The human brain has evolved over many thousands of years, yet only in the last 100, a blip in that timeline, have we demanded that each and every young one sit still and pay attention for 7 hours a day.

Alan Schwartz

In *'ADHD Nation'* (2016), Alan Schwartz dives into the history of Attention Deficit Hyperactivity Disorder (ADHD). He explains that the ADHD brain does not look any different to a neurotypical brain when scanned but that diagnosis is instead about fulfilling a set of behavioural criteria and embodying a collection of symptoms.

We weirdly believe that sitting still obediently is a reflection of human health. In the 1960s, Dr Keith Conners was the first to step forward with the solution - bring in the drugs! At this point, the 'disorder' was known as *minimal brain dysfunction*. I've always found the distinction between legal and illegal drugs a weird one. I grew up around alcohol use and saw the ways people would distort and become aggressive. I watched my grandma pour away hemp milk when she realised it was from the cannabis plant before taking the handful of pills she takes every day to remain well. I've experimented with almost every illegal drug on the market and had a lot of fun, reaching heights of happiness, connection and aliveness incomprehensible before (and experienced the polarity of that, too!). At the ripe old age of 30, my wild party days are now firmly behind me, though I am partial to the occasional glass of red wine. Though things got hella dark at points, I'm glad I played in my youth.

The pharmaceutical industry is one of the most profitable industries in the world alongside oil and arms. Statista estimated its total worth at 1.42 trillion US dollars at the end of 2021. *Aspirin* sales alone rake in half a billion dollars every year and *Bayer*, the company responsible for it, once genuinely marketed heroin as a morphine substitute/cough suppressant without risk of addiction. Say what!? Interestingly, pharma companies invest most of their money into promotion and marketing, not research or drug development. Schwartz' book also shared some of the ridiculously twisted to the point of hilarious advertising campaigns, such as:

> RITALIN: helps the 'problem child' become lovable again.

Despite side effects like sleeplessness, loss of appetite, anxiety, suicidal thoughts and drug-induced psychosis, Keith Conners decided to start prescribing *Ritalin* (a kind of amphetamine) to children as he noticed that it curbed their tendency to run around and helped them focus.

Amphetamines are now a class B drug in the UK and if you're caught with them, you could wind up in prison for five years, unless they've been prescribed by a doctor. Amphetamines were legal for a long while, though. Churchill dosed 72 million British soldiers up on Benzedrine in the Second World War, many of them were tripping their way through their service! In the 1970s, arguably the height of recreational drug culture, it was not weed, LSD or heroin that had the most users: it was Dexedrine. In Vietnam, 7% of the soldiers came away as amphetamine addicts following a prescription of Dexedrine they received in their rations. Then there's the diet pill phase where hundreds of thousands of people were given speed (methamphetamine) to curb their appetite and lose weight, developing serious addictions and having horrendous hallucinations. *'Requiem for a Dream'* (2000) is a powerfully disturbing film which highlights these issues. I remember back in my party days there was a bit of a speed (amphetamine) craze. I went round to a friend's house and found him playing 'Tetris' on the computer, where he had been for five days straight without sleep. He was IN. It for sure helps you focus! But at what cost? It is ridiculously easy to get hooked.

By 1989, parents were noticing the horrible side effects of Ritalin for their children and the lawsuits against the pharmaceutical company were mounting up. Other doctors were up in arms. Dr Peter Breggin famously referred to the Ritalin kids as 'good, caged animals.' Around the same time, however, parents were rallying together to get an official diagnosis for their kids and CHADD (Children with Attention Deficit Disorder) was formed to fight for ADD to be recognised officially as a learning disability. The group made huge waves but fell into disarray when it was discovered that the campaign had been funded by CIBA, the manufacturers of Ritalin. Of course, it was well within their interests to define ADD as an official illness as they had the patented magic cure. By 1990, Ritalin sales had gone up by 400%.

The other piece in this picture is that Ritalin and other similar drugs like Adderall not only help you focus but they get you good grades, too. Kids quickly cottoned on to this and there are a crazy number of cases where children blagged their way through the doctor's consults to get their hands on pills. It's so easy. And with the ever-mounting pressure on kids to academically succeed, it's no surprise really. My best assignment at university the first time round was chemically supported. I'd run out of time for an assignment, so I bought a bag, locked myself in my room and smashed out an essay in a couple of days without sleep. It was my highest-ranking grade and I came top of the class.

At present, 15% of American kids are diagnosed with ADHD and 3% of kids are diagnosed with autism, which for me begs the question: what **is** neuro-normality? If we are unable to submit or adhere to social norms, we are seen as deficient in some way. I'm watching more and more of my adult friends being diagnosed as neurodiverse, and to be honest, if I was to go through an assessment, I would no doubt be part of the gang, too. When I'm studying or writing, I need a very particular environment and get to a certain point where I have to stand up and move around, which is actually when I have a little dance. I'm insanely sensitive to loud noises, especially when they are unexpected, and often get triggered into meltdowns in response. I have to put everything into my diary with an alarm set an hour before it happens or I don't remember. I do 20 tasks simultaneously, especially when it's stuff I'm not super passionate about but need to get done. When I'm cleaning, I'll fill the sink up whilst tidying away whatever I've thrown on the floor at the same time as cleaning the bathroom, before coming back to the now cold washing up water to clean a few things before dashing to put a clothes wash on and start hoovering. I've lived in 19 homes and I'm 30 years old. I can skim-read a 300 page book in an hour. I sometimes get overwhelmed and burned out to the point of not being able to leave my bed. If I don't care about something and I'm not invested, I literally can't do it, but I get obsessed with subjects I am interested in and want to talk about them all the time.

I guess the difference for me is that I've created a life and world that doesn't ask me to be any different. I've been self-employed for most of my adult life and I'm (just about) able to make money with all my quirks still intact. In fact, I've probably been able to create a business that suits me because of my quirks. I know not everyone has that privilege.

I struggle to support the idea of normality in any realm of life but I do feel that there are different operating systems when it comes to people's minds. We need to move away from the idea of 'not normal' and focus on what each individual needs to thrive. What we deem as 'normal' seems to be more about subservience, not health and wellbeing. Instead of drugging children to adapt to an environment that doesn't suit their neurological and behavioural tendencies, maybe we can find the environment that does suit them? Our role as adults is to support kids to find ways of being in the world as themselves.

One of the boldest characters I met during my research was a young lad who had an ADHD diagnosis. He spoke at 1000 miles an hour, lit up each and every room he went into and loved pushing the boundaries of social norms. I have no idea what would have happened to him if he was in a mainstream setting. He really thrived in the self-directed space; he was able to bounce off the walls and tinker with things until he moved on to something else, and had already decided he was going to be a gamer. He loved video games. Not only was he good at them but he was also a hilarious narrator. The school allowed him to be himself and celebrated him for it. He didn't need to be sedated as nobody was trying to control him or his behaviour.

Autism

From a more spiritual perspective, I feel that autism is about sensitivity. These young people feel everything in our harsh world more than the rest of humanity and have to dissociate somewhat to deal with that. Whether that is about 'being in their own world' or being plugged into devices, they have different needs. They also don't adhere to the performed social norms that the rest of people are conditioned to uphold, which I love and respect! We all deserve to have loving and deep relationships, though, and often in order to cultivate these with young people that have autism, we have to join them in their worlds. We have to sit on the edge of their experience and meet them there.

There was a young boy with autism at one of the schools I visited, and I don't think this set up actually suited him. He was often playing alone, happily, but he also couldn't comprehend the very few rules in the space about staying safe. He didn't communicate in traditional ways and you kind of had to put in effort to connect with him. Whilst I was there, I had a beautiful breakthrough with him - a whole hour of sandpit adventures that began when I started mirroring his play. Over and over, we built a big sandcastle. It was simple, repetitive, connected and ours. At one point, he even looked me in the eye! This is a really big thing for kids with autism and an absolute privilege to receive. Without direct intervention, though, kids like this can go through their whole lives without truly interacting with others.

Another kid I met during my research would have had a diagnosis if it had been pursued, but instead, they were just plugged into a device all the time. And I really get it. I can't do public spaces without my headphones on. It overwhelms me. I'm working on it but it often feels physically painful to be in such a stimulating and chaotic environment. I have lots of really nourishing relationships, though. I spend time in deep connection with others in spaces that feel calm and peaceful. Though having coping mechanisms for sensitive children is key, I feel like it's doing a disservice to them to not be actively building bridges to support them to find their way of being in relationships, and in the world, too.

I also witnessed how labelling can become an excuse for certain behaviours, from the kids themselves or from the parents. The challenge of having boundaries with kids prone to huge meltdowns is hardcore, but it is important. Having a limit on screen time or sugar or having to share and compromise in relating with others is hard for all humans, especially when their will is developing. Regardless of how intense our triggers are, we all need boundaries. It's not okay to get violent if you don't get your own way. It's not okay to receive violence if your kid doesn't get their own way. And allowing these things because of a diagnosis is creating so much more harm in the long run.

Boundaries are the key to successful relating and being safe in the world. If it feels hard to enforce them, that's more about us than the kids. We're all in the pot of learning about relationships and it's super easy to excuse things when we have a reason, whether that's our personal trauma, a diagnosis or any other variable. Everyone has their quirks and we will all remain in progress throughout our lives. The important piece is that we continue to love ourselves and one another into the best versions of ourselves. We all need different things to enable that; it's not about 'equality' and everyone receiving the same, it's about 'equity' where everybody gets what they need individually, to blossom into themselves. Neurodiverse people have different needs but the foundations of forming loving relationships remain the same.

All kids are individual people with specific needs and interests. Sometimes what is empowering for one - for example, a space where they are free to be self-directed - can be isolating or limiting for another. Some children need intervention to flourish and that is okay. What will suit one kid with ADHD or autism might not suit another with the same diagnosis. It is so important to get to know children individually instead of assuming we know who they are and what they need because of the label they've been given, whether that's about brain wiring, body ability, race, gender, age or sexuality. The beautiful thing about the schools I visited was that there really was space for individuality. Kids weren't rejected or bullied because of their neurological status; it was just an aspect of their personality that was welcomed and celebrated.

ORGANISATION

The self-directed philosophy trusts children, believing that learning is natural and happens best when people are making their own decisions and following their interests. Though both the communities I visited in the States were democratic and self-directed, the systems and tools they functioned through were very different.

In my eyes, Sudbury schools were part of the first wave of the reclamation of self-direction (we are a historically self-directed species, evolving for THOUSANDS of years without poking and prodding). Birthed in the 1960s, the Sudbury model followed Summerhill in creating opportunities for young people to guide and direct their own learning experiences. Today, there are more than 60 Sudbury schools across the world and the focus is on autonomy above all else. There is no kind of taught intervention; adults in the space are there to respond to invitations from the kids and facilitate the democratic decision-making process.

Agile Learning Centres (ALCs) are young and fresh as they came into being in the 2010s. Building upon all that came before them in terms of self-directed education, they borrow tools from agile software development to enable the philosophy in practice with an additional focus; actively developing a strong and nourishing community. There are around 20 schools established at the time of writing. Though there are more systems in place in ALCs, they aim to streamline processing and provide more space for kids to be following their own flow in a group of others doing the same.

Decision Making

There was a little pot at the Sudbury school filled with notes to be discussed at the upcoming meeting. All were welcome to add to it and anything could be brought to the collective. A group of around four kids along with an adult gathered every day in a room seemingly reserved for the process to discuss what was in the pot. Attendance for this meeting was compulsory and would rotate between all members of the community. The papers would be reviewed and *motions* would be created - people would suggest solutions and actions, which would then be voted upon. I realised recently when watching one of my old favourite TV shows (*'Weeds'*) that the method aligns pretty closely with local governance in the States.

Punishments and school rules came into being through the daily meetings in the Sudbury space to ensure that problematic situations would not occur again. Like at Summerhill, there were hundreds of rules that the whole community had co-created in a book. Though they were open for review and adaptation at any time, if a person (adult or child) broke one of the collectively agreed upon rules they would be *written up* and called to a hearing in front of the panel for their punishment to be decided. Often a *privilege* would be revoked. The easiest way to explain privileges is to give you an example. The kids had to go through a mini assessment with an adult to use risky art materials, the first rung of which was about scissors. Once they had the certificate, they could use scissors whilst at school and progress onto the next mini assessment; for instance, to use a glue gun. There were privileges like this for lots of things in the space which could be removed as punishment.

Though the meeting system worked, it was long and arduous. Most of the young people struggled to take it seriously, trapped in a pokey office style room whilst the sun shone outside. I won't lie - two hours into the process, I was also seriously bored. The youngest kids in the meeting were playing under the table, older kids came in and out of the room to try drag us back to '*Super Smash Bros.*' and what I'd have given to join them. I was fighting the urge to throw my Dictaphone out the window in that moment. But I'm a grown-up now, so I just breathed through it and mantra'd the fudge out of 'this too shall pass'. It didn't help that the things being discussed were basically just people grassing one another up for breaking rules. It all felt a bit trivial and the mentor had to really hold the space together.

When I talked about the meetings with some of the adults, they praised it as a real-life example of the laborious process of democracy. It gave the kids an embodied understanding of the political system they lived within and equipped them with the understanding of how to take part in it. I really appreciate this but I noticed that upholding the responsibility to be part of these meetings was compulsory, which didn't really fit with the autonomous piece. Though the intention behind it was about collective responsibility in the present and enabling future political participation, it reflected a strong adult agenda, and my goodness, it was so DRY. It was also a very clear punishment system which I struggled with. 'If you do *x*, you will be punished, so don't do *x*'. The space wasn't provided to dive deeper into what had occurred and why, the focus of the intervention was to decide upon the punishment for doing something 'wrong' and that didn't quite sit right with me.

The method for facilitating the democratic process was simple and quick at the ALC. Inspired by a *Kanban board*, originally created by Toyota, a sheet with four columns was on display in one of the classrooms. The first was an *awareness* column – 'I've noticed this and want to highlight it'. Anyone could add to this section via a post-it note (for example, tidying up at the end of the day); the second column defined the *need* aspect, why it was important (tidying up to take care of the space). Then was the *necessary action steps* section, completed following a discussion (groups being responsible to tidy certain rooms), and the final column was filled in when the issue had been resolved. Issues were kept on the board for a little while to ensure the solution worked long term.

A self-elected group of kids and mentors would meet each week to discuss the *awareness* column and create a streamlined proposal to resolve the issue for the whole school community to then discuss and vote upon. The group was open and each week different kids would show up depending on what was on the agenda. The intention was to get as much sorted in this mini meeting as possible and then feedback in the whole school meeting to make final decisions. It was very clearly about problem-solving and as it was optional, the people in the meetings were really engaged. I chuckled when I heard that one of the busiest meetings had taken place when battles with Nerf guns were being discussed - y'know, the ones that fire little foam bullets?

Sidenote tangent: When I was in my first year of uni, the lads had a phase of BB guns that shot little metal balls (way more painful and risky but still very playful). About a year after the craze had ended, we were sat round getting high and my mate was itching a spot he had on his back. As the picked it, he started absolutely freaking out. He'd unearthed a little BB pellet that had got lodged in there during the battles all those moons ago! It was one of those perfect emotional mixture moments - mind-blowing, hilarious, totally personal to us and the fun we shared together, and absolutely gross.

Anyway, back to Nerf guns and foam bullets that definitely don't break the surface of skin... The kids all showed up at the meeting and the motion passed. They were able to have Nerf wars whenever they wanted! But interestingly, following that meeting, not one Nerf battle took place. It was as if the kids really wanted to have their voices heard and get the permission they desired, but once they had the freedom, it didn't matter anymore. In another little interview, when referencing the democratic process, one kid said, "Everyone, I think, feels very satisfied because they feel they're heard, which is really nice."

Meeting Tools

The ALC had lots of tools to streamline meetings, too. The *gameshifting board* was portable and almost as tall as me. It had different sections like; 'intention' to describe the purpose of the meeting, 'timing' to define when it would start and finish, 'required materials' to help preparation, 'engagement' to explain how people would share during the meeting (taking turns in a circle, putting hands up, just jumping in when they wanted to speak, etc.), amongst other elements. The board described how the meeting would run and was filled in using post-it notes by the 'game master' (the person facilitating) before the meeting began.

The intention with a *gameshifting board* is to make the implicit, explicit and clearly defined. Also integrated with the board were different activities to shake up or bring down the energy of the group; from daft games to mini grounding meditations, questions to stimulate discussions and body check-in prompts; a plethora of tools to meet the needs of the group in that moment and to create the perfect 'vibe' for the intention of the meeting.

The beauty is that once the system was grasped, kids could run meetings themselves. Though they hadn't adopted it in the school I visited, some ALCs use hand signals to communicate with the person speaking during meetings. From signalling their agreement to what is being said, to letting the speaker know that they are repeating themselves or that time is running out, subtle cues can be used to communicate without interrupting flow. Almost like having a secret and incredibly clear language for communication, which I'm sure you'll agree would make life a lot easier.

As mentioned, the kids were split into smaller, age-related groups that would meet each day with a specific mentor. *Band* meetings would open and close the day, facilitating a process that young people would probably use in their lives outside of school; the ability to set an intention and reflect upon it. In morning *band* meetings, everyone was invited to share what they intended for the day; which could be an emotive theme or a specific task - 'What's my plan and how am I gonna do it?' At the end of the day, they would be given the chance to check in with said intention and review their process. A beautiful cycle. I'd love to see something like this integrated into mainstream schools. Instead of everyone having to sit behind their desk for the register, how amazing would it be if the day started with a sharing circle or moment of intention setting that the kids had opportunity to facilitate themselves.

The *band* meeting process at the ALC also lent itself well to the schools gathering 'proof' of children's learning to feedback to authorities that granted them funding. Intentions and reflections are easy to record in a book or online through word, image or another creative method. Though a lot of unschooling parents are fiercely in opposition to such interventions, the local authority can make proof a non-negotiable, so systems like this also double as pretty organic methods of record keeping when it comes to the kids' creative and learning processes.

I recently found a cool Facebook group called, *'What my unschooler is learning when…'* which may be helpful for tracking learning. People ask questions like, "What is my kiddo learning when she watches Simpson's all day," or "What is my 10 year old daughter learning when she takes care of a baby pigeon?". The community of over 10,000 parents then work together to identify what the child is learning, helping the family to articulate how they are meeting local authority learning objectives through children's self-directed activities.

Structure and Flow

To be able to flow and create both individually and collaboratively, we need structure. But too much structure drains our juice. It's a fine line to tow. The ALC, as you're probably piecing together, was really good at this.

In the central point of the L-shaped building was a big *set the week board*, a timetable of things on offer in the space that kids could attend if they chose to. It was rich, varied and felt exciting. There were so many different activities on offer! From group games to academic topics like mathematics and science, to robotics, movie watching, book reading, soap making, aerial silks, farm chores, bug hunting, cooking, textiles, drumming, dancing, theatre and so much more. Some offerings were one-offs, others happened every week, some were part of a series. Anyone could attend any session; they were accessible for all ages and ability levels. A buffet of delicious opportunity facilitated by people that were super passionate about what they were sharing. There were organic sessions that opened in the moment; a kid would ask for help with something and a group would spontaneously huddle round a mentor as they learned a new skill. Tutors also came in and out of the space to help kids with exams they might want to pursue. The schedule was full and the environment was incredibly well resourced, if kids weren't in a facilitated session, they would often be found diving deep into their own projects, with floating mentors on hand to support them to bring their intentions and desires into fruition.

Though the week was full to the brim with opportunity, the only thing kids had to attend were *band* meetings. The rest of the time, they were free to follow their own flow, even if that meant doing 'nothing.' In my opinion there is no such thing as doing nothing. When we are not gathering more information or experience, we are usually processing or integrating what has already happened. Rest is so valuable and important (contrary to the capitalist narrative), just look at what we need when we are sick.

Band meetings and the *set the week board* offered kids a sense of rhythm. The amazing playworker I mentioned at the start of the book, Fraser Brown, would always wow us in lectures. I remember him once talking about rhythm from a play perspective. He shared that our first experience upon conception is marked by rhythm - the beat of our mother's heart. We are naturally rhythmic beings. Having our day scheduled without any space for free unscripted time is ultimately smothering and usually results in dis-ease. But routine and rhythm interspersed around free moment living supports all manner of things, including self-regulation. A friend of mine who is a Kundalini yoga teacher and life student once shared with me that no matter where he is in the world, no matter how stormy or exciting his life and experiences might get, when he sits on his mat each morning, he comes home. He returns to centre. He reboots. Routine supports us to anchor.

Conflict Resolution

The human body is 90% water, so we're basically cucumbers with anxiety.

Anon

One of the few times I managed to blur into the background, I saw a group of kids gathered round the table that had Lego boards permanently glued to it. There were five of them, between six and eight years old, playing together and some kind of conflict broke out. "I think you should give it back," one child stated. The rest agreed with him. I peeped over my papers to see the kid in question blush and return the piece of Lego. No adults were called into the situation; they sorted it out themselves.

This experience made me think of what A. S. Neill noticed. When children in mainstream school are taken to the authority figure for their punishment to be dealt, it happens in secret and the biggest threat is what mum and dad will say. The worst-case scenario in a democratic school is that it will be taken to the community meeting, where all your mates and teachers will find out what happened and be involved in what happens next. There's nowhere to hide. The kids know they aren't gonna be 'saved' by adults and therefore it's in everyone's interest to handle conflict in the moment, speaking the truth, taking responsibility and allowing these little experiences to be resolved as quickly as they emerge. I feel this is made more accessible because there isn't a cultivation of dependency upon external forces to swoop in, due to the conscious removal of hierarchy in the space. Kids are trusted and given the opportunity to learn from the direct experience of their relating, as opposed to being shamed or punished by an external person that wasn't directly involved in the situation.

The other thing to note here is just how corrupting these forced apologies we demand from kids actually are. Someone being manipulated into an empty 'sorry' does not embody responsibility or genuine emotion; it is a meaningless charade. When people, never mind children, are given the space and indeed the tools to truly reflect upon their actions and receive the other person's response to said actions, they are much more likely to feel remorse and learn from the experience, whether they communicate it or not. The performance of feigned responsibility we expect from kids (and celebrate them for, "Well done for saying sorry, you can go and play now.") does not establish a healthy foundation for relating. It creates a culture of avoidance and falseness. I have met few people that can truly take responsibility or genuinely apologise when they've behaved in ways that have crossed another's boundaries - I wonder if that would be the same if we weren't forced to say sorry as punishment when we were children?

Instead of 'behaviour management' at the schools, everything was about the navigation of boundaries. Having respect at the core of these conversations changes everything. It's not about teaching children to 'be good' or not upset people; it's about them figuring out where they end and the other begins, knowing their place within relationships and the wider community. So often we intervene in a child's behaviour to 'tell them off', but what is that very defined point of interjection? In that moment, it's usually fear-stimulated and often related to judgement. What other people will think about them and us as a result of that behaviour. We all have to learn in one way or another about the needs and boundaries of ourselves and everyone else. We have an opportunity to process with kids in the same way that we do in our adult relationships, and I tell you what, when we really lean in to evolving consciously with children, it's not just them that reap the benefits.

The ALC had a specific system for processing conflict inspired by the *non-violent communication* (NVC) model. Focusing on the expression of facts along with ownership of emotions meant there was less space for arguments and people getting hurt. The process was guided by four questions: *'what happened?'* which was to be explored without judgement or blame, *'how do you feel about what happened?',* followed by *'what do you need to move forward?'*. The process would then be completed with *'what can we agree to?'*. Along with the queries, there were three tiers of the process. Hopefully, as was reflected in the Lego situation, a simple conversation between the people involved would resolve the conflict. If not, the next step was to work through the enquiries with a third party to act as somewhat of a meditator, whether another child or an adult. If this still didn't resolve the issue, the conflict could be taken to the school meeting to be resolved by the group. Again, the streamlined process meant that, if possible, things could resolve quickly.

This is another example of a lived experience that children often don't have the opportunity to access. The reward and punishment system often presented when external people step in to 'sort kids out' does not work in adult relationships. Though we may have space held for us to process, nobody is gonna step in and sort things out for us. Learning to stick to facts and needs is such a gift for young people. Most of us have learned to have shadowy, blame-filled tantrums or play games of avoidance and gaslighting which prevent us from really meeting each other (I'm definitely still in process with this and I believe the majority of us are). If we use conscious systems with kids, these models of relating become the embodied operating system for how they do relationships. Like all the systems in the ALC, the conflict resolution model wasn't just for the children. Whether it was a meeting or situation between parents, mentors, kids or a mixture of everyone, the tools of the culture were used by the whole community.

Emotional Processing

We've recently had phenomenal growth in the realms of technology and industry, perhaps even in intellect, too, but we're only just starting to scratch the surface with emotional navigation. Generally, the adults of today were not raised in 'conscious' spaces where there was permission to be honest or the tools available to calm themselves. I read somewhere once that the fight/flight/freeze mechanism in the human fires the exact same way as it would if we were up against a sabretooth tiger, when we now have conflict in our comfy little kitchens about who's going to do the washing up. We are dealing with ancient parts of ourselves that have not yet caught up to the safety most of us exist within. Not only that, because it's rare to find someone that has been given emotional permission, most of us have no idea what we are really feeling, never mind an ability to communicate it.

Another category of the fight/flight/freeze mechanism has recently been mapped called *fawning*. Roll over, be kind, be nice, please and you'll survive. It's not a conscious process; these trauma responses come from a space inside us that the intellect cannot control (or perceive). But the sticky thing with the *fawn* response is that it is celebrated in our culture. Dissociating from our feelings and popping on a smile is seen as being the 'bigger person' but being unable to say no and set boundaries is actually a very dangerous space to inhabit. I was stuck in fawn for many years and found myself in numerous destructive situations as a result. Looking back on it now, I can feel the sensation of how I'd go from freeze into fawn. I was once sexually assaulted by a male masseuse. After the experience, I got up, shaking and frightened out of my wits but being as sweet as I possibly could be. I actually fricking paid him before running back to the apartment I was staying in. These 'good girl/boy' conditionings can morph in some very toxic ways.

When big emotions come up, we usually either project them out and hurt other people or we learn to suppress them. Our world is a theme park of opportunities for suppression. Whether we use illegal substances or ride the household drug waves with sugar, caffeine, alcohol and over the counter medicine, we put something **in** to change how we feel. Suppress the conflict, suppress the emotion, suppress the discomfort, brush it all under the rug and return to 'harmony'. But when we suppress, we get clogged up and eventually these things come back to bite us. We aren't comfortable with our own pain and emotions, and so we struggle to give other people the space to have their emotional experience, too.

I find it fascinating to witness younger children in their tantrums. I've been through a huge journey of dissociation and numbing; and when I stopped doing that, I realised that big emotions need to be let out. When I feel big feels, I need to shout and scream, vocally expressing. I need to shake my body and stamp my feet. I need to let the pain move. And something profound happens when we let it. In the beginning, it was a messy process and I sometimes ended up directing the energy that was moving through me at people I loved, which I deeply regret, but recognise it now as a part of the thawing and 'learning how to feel' process. These days, I exist in a community with people that value opportunities to emotionally release and have spaces with loud, tribal music where I can shout, scream, stamp, stretch and release, whilst being held in love, as others go through their own processes, too.

I know we all think being a grown-up is hard, but if we allow ourselves to feel in, being a kid must be really challenging. You start to have your own desires and drivers but there's this bigger human that says no all the time. I'm not saying that we shouldn't, either, especially considering that toddlers have almost no ability to assess risk, understand how much things cost and all the other factors, but what I'm attempting to highlight is that it sucks to not be able to exercise your own will. We damn the resulting expression as an immature 'tantrum' but maybe what we are seeing is an innate ability to emotionally process. It makes me laugh that these outbursts often happen in public in places like the supermarket for all to see and hear (and judge). C'mon, though - you're a kid, you love sugar, marketing companies know how to push buttons of desire, and so everything is crazy colourful and appealing, but you're not allowed any of it!

Another amazing video doing the rounds on social media over the past few years was of a dad holding space for his toddler who was having a meltdown. He simply sat with the little bambino for as long as it took. In some moments, the bean was screaming and punching and pushing, then at other times they were sobbing and snuggling, but dad never turned his back. He sat there with open arms and held space for the processing. What a gift. How different things would be if we were open to the normality of intense emotions and made space for them in our relationships.

In one of the classrooms, a little girl wandered in clearly very upset. The mentors reassured her that mommy would be coming soon but they didn't rush in to cuddle or comfort. I found that really hard to sit with, but as I dropped deeper into exploring what was going on for me, I saw the ways in which her distress was triggering *me,* and I wanted to stop it. She eventually calmed down and went back to playing happily. What would have happened if the adults swooped in to rescue her from her own emotions? Through that little experience, she was given the space and opportunity to self soothe. She wasn't banished from connection (like in the instance of locking babies in separate rooms in their cots to cry themselves to sleep) and everyone was still very much available to interact with, but because she was given the space to experience her emotion, she seemed to process without depending upon another to soothe her.

Often in traditional school settings, teachers don't have the space or opportunity to regulate themselves, either. Their to-do list and never ending list of responsibilities means that they often have no bandwidth left. Most teachers I know have burned out and exited the profession. And I don't blame them. I couldn't do it. You are expected to dissociate from your own life, body, challenges and emotions to show up as 'teacher' for the children. This in itself creates a discord within the environment. When someone is holding in their emotions to keep their shit together, everyone can feel it. One of the mentors really highlighted this piece during an interview and it struck me deeply - if staff are 'triggered' and in fight or flight mode, how can they possibly facilitate positive experiences for young people?

It's difficult to imagine how this could change in mainstream schools. The weird set up means that if kids are in the hella controlling classroom environment without the teacher, their wild selves explode into a desire to break all the rules. A triggered teacher saying, "I just need a minute" and leaving the space to calm themselves down, would probably result in chaos. Perhaps a five minute pre-recorded meditation or an activity that guided the whole community to check in with their internal selves and worlds would be more fitting. There are ways we can create space for everybody's emotions in classrooms, but it's important to note that establishing a culture of two-sided respect and trust takes time and is almost impossible when the vibe reeks of a dictatorship.

If there is space in schools for adults to connect to themselves and return to centre when they wobble, the environment and flow feels better for everyone. Not only that but it offers a living transmission of what it is to be human. I long to see a world where everyone is living as their authentic selves in all of their relationships. How different life would be if we could just drop the masks.

PARENTAL INVOLVEMENT

The dynamic between parents and the adults that work with their kids is interesting to say the least. Again, because our abilities to communicate are not yet operating on all cylinders, things when undefined can become foggy and this is where projections take hold. The expectation of what a 'teacher' will provide for your kids is probably different for everyone and this creates a bit of a minefield.

The schools I visited defined very clearly what the space (and adults) would and wouldn't provide. One of the founders shared with me the challenge of wanting to make the school's philosophy fit the needs of every family, especially when they were first opening. When parents would express interest, they tried to find ways that the school could bend to meet them, but eventually they realised they just couldn't. It's so tempting to dilute or distort what we truly desire to create in order to get clients, customers, students or funding, but getting really clear on the definition and intentions of what we are offering will attract the right people. If not, the whole purpose of the endeavour gets blurred and watered down, no longer existing in the way it was intended.

A big element of both the ALC and the Sudbury school (due to the nature of their approach) was to support parents to feel safe and in alignment with self-directed learning. There were regular meetings, where research and recommended reading would be offered, along with the opportunity to process and ask questions. They didn't expect parents to blindly trust the radical notions the schools were built upon and were there to hold space for the challenges, struggles and the fear, too. But the self-directed philosophy would not be adapted in response to any of those things, no matter what came up. The fabric of the space would not be compromised.

I met a woman recently who sent her daughter to a democratic school in the UK. It was clear that she had an expectation that, at some point when her daughter was a teenager, the school would begin to prepare her for formal examinations. She was frustrated and disappointed that this wasn't happening, but knowing the democratic philosophy, I would have been very surprised if this was a component of the school. Would she have enrolled her daughter at the school if she'd known there would be no preparation for exams? Perhaps not.

Steiner schools also have an interesting relationship with parental involvement. They aren't forthcoming about the learning philosophy but protect it fiercely. Parents are not allowed to be involved in running the schools and boards are made up of Anthroposophists and teachers to ensure that the schools stay aligned with Steiner's intentions. And in some ways, I get it - parents naturally focus on what they perceive *their* kids need and the wider educational philosophy or larger group needs are secondary.

Helicopter parenting references the modern approach to childrearing. Parents hover over their kids, micro-managing their every action, wanting to be involved in everything that they do (and think, and feel). It makes me smile because often parents that exist like this wear it as a badge of honour, but really, it's stimulated by anxiety and a need for control, which can really harm kids in the long run. When parents are wanting to do things 'right' for their kids, it's quite easy to drop into that mode. I'm a playworker and champion self-direction to the nth degree, but when my little cousins are getting well risky in their play, I want to throw up! The fear is real but it is our own.

If you don't want to take the mainstream path, it's important to get clear about the philosophies you align with. Recognising what the needs are for your kids as individual beings, and for you guys as a family, must come before you start looking for projects, schools or people to collaborate with. Once this is defined, I guarantee that you'll find the right people or place, because on an energetic level, you are crystal clear in your intention. With everything we do in life, if we start with self-enquiry and get clear individually first, we know what we are looking for and thus find it. But as is the case with all aspects of raising children (and life), it will be a constant process of letting go of control and learning to soften when you want to hold on tighter.

This makes me think of the first time I rode a scooter. I was in India, it was dark, I was in a new place and I was lost. I hit the curb, lost control and instead of softening and letting go, I clutched on to the accelerator, twisting like there was no tomorrow and mangling my leg in the meantime. When we are frightened, we cling on, but often that's precisely the moment we need to let the fudge go and allow the wave to crash.

PROGRESSION

The young do not know enough to be prudent, and therefore they attempt the impossible, and achieve it, generation after generation.

Pablo Picasso

Earlier in the book, I introduced you to the notion of the *being child*: kids being valued here and now. The opposite of this is the *becoming child,* the mainstream way of looking at kids, where we see and value them according to what we want them to become in the future. This is something I've witnessed many times when it comes to schooling. Parents quite rightly don't want to rob their children of opportunities. Though more radical approaches might seem attractive, the stumbling block for many is the fear of limiting what comes next. Especially when it comes to education post 11 years old, the risk feels too heavily weighted and children often end up at mainstream school as a result. This is ironic and tragic, as high school is where the dictatorship model really takes hold.

Removing compulsion from learning does not prevent kids from taking exams or getting qualifications.

Really sit with that for a moment and let it sink in.

Kids in mainstream school have a stick up their butt throughout their education journey, pushing them into compulsory examinations. For a lot of children, this damages their mental health and puts pressure upon them that paradoxically negatively affects their grades. When we get to university education, the model totally shifts. It becomes self-directed. Young people are given the reigns. You get your timetable and it is down to you to attend lectures, take notes and study for exams... Or not. Somehow, in our weird ways of seeing things, we've decide that before 18 years old, humans are not mature enough to handle this responsibility.

I don't think I know anyone who knew what they wanted to do with their lives following school. And it was the same at university. We'd been coerced and forced instead of given the opportunity to explore ourselves and what we really liked. Quite a few of my friends have settled overseas doing minimum wage jobs to sustain their adventurous lifestyles. Others are coasting here in the UK working in offices to maintain the expense of living. The happiest people I know are self-employed creatives that either developed their skillset outside of formal education or returned to school when they were in their mid-twenties after figuring themselves and life out a bit. Some of my friends have made loads of money and their names are known all over the world, not because of what they studied, but because they found themselves and their niche.

I saw a lot of inspired and motivated people during my research that weren't being pushed. When you've been allowed to direct yourself, you learn that, ultimately, it will always be down to you. If the kids wanted to go to college, they knew they'd need to work to get there. Just like everyone else. Some of them had tutors outside of school. But the subtle difference here is about consent. They said they wanted it and so it happened. No forced, pinned to the table, manipulation tactics needed. The eldest student I met had just aced his SAT examination and was going to the college of his choosing.

What if childhood was an opportunity to discover what makes us happy and develop the skills we need to pursue our fulfilment?

A friend of mine unschooled her daughter and as she grew, it turned out that one of her superpowers was drawing. As the years passed, she almost accidentally developed a portfolio of her work. At 16, she decided that she wanted to go to a sixth form college. She showed them her work; they were wowed and offered her a place straight away. This story was reflected with a couple of the students I met during my research and with some Steiner students I've met over the years, too. Their creative portfolios granted them entrance into the institution. And, their applications and interviews were often deeply celebrated because of the levels of self-motivation, creativity and individuality they demonstrated. Oh, and the dropout rate for kids like this is phenomenally lower than kids coming straight from mainstream schools. Their true, passionate selves are already switched on!

We have to remember that young people are human, just like us. If trauma doesn't prevent it, when we decide we want to do something, we pull our socks up and we make it happen. Even if that means going back to school when we are 50 years old and figuring out how to fit into academia. Even if we have to work a job we don't really like to save up the money for a plane ticket. The choices we make when we are 12 or even 30 years old aren't as important as we all fearfully project. Life is a continuum of experience within which we change, develop and explore.

Another thing to note is that kids are growing up in different ways to life before the internet. There is more access to what the 'real world' is about through things like social media and YouTube. The limitations of childhood are easier for young people to recognise, even if they can't conceptualise the experience. Speaking to some of the older kids during my research, I found that many of them had ended up in these radical spaces because of mental health issues. They'd become seriously depressed and couldn't hack mainstream schooling - a common experience these days. Forcing kids to stay in school to 'keep their options open' can often destroy the essential things required to access those options, things like positive mental health, drive and inspiration.

I follow a phenomenal home-educated young woman on Facebook called Meka. Her page is called 'Mindfulness with Meka'. She's no older than 12 and she is a yoga teacher! Her (very unspiritual) parents let her lead and when she said she wanted to do a yoga qualification a few years ago, they let her pursue it. She's now social media famous, influencing and inspiring adults and children alike, running circles to support young women to enter into their first bleed without shame, and supporting her peers to drop into their bodies through her super-duper yoga classes. I know that she's an anomaly but she's a living example of how kids can fulfil their potential even when they are still children, simply through being allowed to follow their passions.

Let's stop all this focus on what will happen in the future for kids and start trusting them to find their way through life, collaborating with them to change the landscape of childhood. Very few people follow the path their parents suggest and end up fulfilled. That formula doesn't work, let's stop repeating it. Our responsibility is to support kids to explore themselves and the world, finding the spaces that feel like a fit for them. The skills we really need aren't taught in school anyway. Being treated like cattle causes seriously messy things within us. And it doesn't have to be like that. Meka is a shining example.

MAKING THE LEAP

Okay, so you're feeling all inspired with potentiality. But where the flipperty flop do you begin when it comes to making different choices for kids' education?

First up, you gotta deal with that fear! We are saturated with limitation. It's part of the bag of being human. Anything we create outwardly is flavoured by what is inside of us. For better or for worse. Though I have offered examples throughout the book to support you to step off the conveyor belt, if we don't do the *inner work* to dismantle our fears, we can't move forward differently.

Self-enquiry is the first step. Sit with your own feelings, thoughts and fears about education and then question where they came from. Are you hearing your parents' voices in your head? Or is it a schoolteacher? Perhaps these ideas are conclusions you came to after a difficult experience that you or someone around you had in relation to school? Dig and find the roots, then fact-check your brain! Is what you're thinking really true in the present?

Sometimes, the internal fact-checking process is enough to pop us out of untruth. But at other times, there's trauma held in our bodies that needs to be released. Maybe the tears of your nine year old self were never permitted to be cried. Perhaps the fear response from being punished by caregivers got stuck and needs to be shaken out. Potentially, you're throwing the baby out with the bath water 'cause you were pushed way too hard and actually you need to scream all that rage out. Or it might be a gripping fear of rejection from your family and friends that needs some loving intervention.

There are many tools out there to support us to process our feelings. And then, from a clear space, we're able to tune in to what the children in our care need because we've got ourselves feeling safe and therefore aren't projecting anymore. Rest assured that everyone that I've met doing things a bit differently has moments of doubt. Once we've got the map of our internal world, though, we're less likely to react and push/pull kids accordingly. We can check our map, recognise what historic pain is popping off, soothe that part of ourselves and then re-find our feet and centre without dragging kids into the storm with us.

GRASSROOTS COLLABORATION

There is space for us to create different experiences for children outside of the system. If a group of home educators combine forces, you have a team of people able to share and collaborate. This could be a cluster of 10 families sharing responsibility for the kids. Three adults each day facilitating from someone's living room, a public woodland or a beach. It doesn't have to be big. It doesn't have to be official. It doesn't have to be a full-time job for anyone involved and also overcomes the biggest issue I have with home education; the lack of community for the kids.

For this to work, though, you need to be clear about what it is you want for your family and create agreements with the people you are collaborating with before anything begins. This model relies heavily on parental involvement, which can make things tricky but utilising the agile tools I've described, along with bringing in an external person to guide you can help create a well-defined, solid foundation and culture (and avoid the sticky trap of codependency between parents and their kids). The key to this and any co-creation is GOOD RELATIONSHIPS. If you don't have that, it ain't gonna work. But if you lock in the processes for conflict harmonisation and decision making in the very early stages, you've got a fighting chance. Start with each person getting clear about their heart seeds and non-negotiables, followed by some desires that are more flexible and if these ideals seem to align, create your system for collaborating. Make sure everyone has opted in to the collectively agreed 'this is how we relate here' process before you start planning or actioning things. The rest of the pieces fall into place when the social fabric is sparkly. And then, like I've said, it's all about letting go. Have a look at the ALC website noted at the back of the book for some fantastic resources.

If you want to set up something a little bigger, many festival sites are not used through the winter. Get a few bell tents with burners and some solar power and you're cooking on gas. The cost is kept down. It's gentle for the environment. Humans are anchored back into the ecosystem, consciously. It isn't an official system and therefore doesn't need to be overseen by a governing body. There is even scope for families to get nomadic with it, too. Travelling from location to location and setting up temporary spaces where adults and kids can trade skills, time, resources and money.

When we really begin to deconstruct what we have been taught about life and what is possible, there is so much opportunity to create alternative ways of being, relating and educating our kids. There is scope for creating radical things without the need to buy land (how we could possibly ever *own* land is beyond me...) or spend loads of money to rent a building and everything that comes with that. It all comes down to community co-creation.

If you want to open an official school, it gets a little more bureaucratic. You'll need to consider insurance and child/adult ratios, risk assessments, policies and criminal record checks, funding, accountancy and how you will meet what the local authority expects you to deliver as an 'education establishment'. I love that so many parents and educators are creating radical opportunities for children, but class and access are big issues for me. Every young person deserves a childhood that supports them to flourish into the best version of themselves. Every young person deserves the opportunity to create a happy, healthy life for themselves. Every young person deserves to be seen, celebrated, valued and loved.

I want to see a world where families get to choose from a variety of state funded schools with differing approaches and philosophies, so that each child can find their perfect fit. That feels far, far away at the moment but you and I changing the way we see and respond to kids is something we can do right now. Whether that's a tiny shift within our family, creating space for autonomy in our classroom, or creating a new learning centre, we don't have to do it all, we don't have to do it alone and we can approach it playfully! Kids can help us return to the remembrance that life is extraordinary. When we create more space for that feeling of 'wow, life is really something special', our hearts get to breathe. And when our hearts get to breathe, our passion comes online. And when our passion comes online, we find our piece, our peace and our people.

CONCLUDING THOUGHTS

Y'know what the driver is for most of us snowflakes? We wanna change the world. We wanna make things better. For me, it's always been about children. Creating space in childhood for more autonomy because children deserve it <u>and</u> because I want to see grown up people feeling free to make their own decisions. The more space we have in our conditioning, the more creative we can be. Creativity feels really good inside of us and is also a key skill for problem solving. And we all know that humanity has got some problems to solve!

My intention for this writing is to encourage questioning and to share inspiration, highlighting issues and introducing solutions. I've shared insight into alternative systems like Steiner, Krishnamurti, Montessori, project-based learning and various threads of the democratic education model, in the hopes that you can identify the elements of each that would suit the learning needs of young people in your care. If you're creating your own approach at home or in a classroom, cut and paste what works with your child or group.

We can create rich environments with inspirational and diverse adults where children's culture can be explored and lived, inclusive of all, with awesome systems for relating and creating. It doesn't have to be a school where all these elements pop off at once, it's about crafting a life for kids that include all those things. <u>Childhood is education</u>. It's not about a specific system or a special place, it's the whole kit and kaboodle. How can you support the kids around you to access more of this good stuff?

People-led change is possible and has happened throughout history, remarkably so in the past few hundred years. Can you imagine how it must have felt to be suddenly free after the 13th amendment was adopted in the US? How elating it must have felt as a woman to vote for the first time? Somehow, little by little and then all at once, change happens.

Maybe education reform isn't about overhauling the system, maybe it's about tiny changes that loads of people make. These little changes will have a huge effect on the young people in our lives and in my opinion, that is more than enough.

It's down to you and me, beloveds.

What are *you* gonna do about school?

MY PART IN THE SHIFT

I've personally had a love/hate relationship with formal education. I've always been classified as bright and able, yet also identified as rebellious and struggling with authority. At prom when graduating from secondary school, I received two awards: 'Little Miss Bad' and 'Most Controversial Person'.

I distinctly remember the feeling of entering 'The 5,5,5 Club' (the highest grades possible for SATs at 11 years old in the UK). I received a t-shirt with special embroidery on and my chest swelled with pride. I also distinctly remember opening the letter which revealed that I had failed the majority of my GCSE exams when I was 16 years old. For that, I received a crushed spirit and an internalised f**k-up badge that took a long time to shake.

I didn't possess the grades or the required effort to progress to A-Levels and refused to enter the world of work, so at 16, I went to sixth form college. I'd moved out of home a few years previous and was existing in the fold of the UK's freeparty scene. I was nourished and taken care of by a community way older than me with a love of music that went as deep as mine did. A family of misfits that fitted together perfectly. So many glorious sunrises next to stacks of speakers during those years.

At college, I did a BTEC national diploma in children's care, learning and development. I was looking for an easy ride to compliment my lifestyle. I discovered that I really did get on with children; they embodied an authenticity that was glaringly missing from the society around me. I didn't get on, however, with the way that adults would stamp on their spirit in the placements I had to do in schools and nurseries. A fire was starting to brew within me.

I had no desire to go to university but my college tutors dragged me to open days, and in Leeds, at the university my mum had spent most of her adult life lecturing from, I found playwork.

I sat in the audience, listening to a talk about the course, feeling validated in a way that had never landed before. These people saw the dynamic between adults and children in the same way that I did. They recognised the distortion. And the playwork field and course existed to do something about it. It was about children's rights, theoretically and practically. I signed up straight away and knew I had found something really significant.

I had my first proper whopper of an experience with synchronicity and divine intervention in my second year of uni. I loved the course content and the tutors, my friends were amazing, as were our adventures, but I was spiralling with drugs. My brain was mashed but I couldn't resist the daily opportunity to get messy. I needed to get out. Somehow, I ended up on the university website and stumbled across an advert. I started crying uncontrollably. The project that my mum had established when she worked at the university was still going strong. She'd gone to India to recruit scholarship students for the events management course she headed up. Whilst there, she visited a project in a slum founded by the father of one of her Indian colleagues. *Sanjay Nagar* supported the reintegration of people that had suffered from leprosy back into the local community. Though leprosy had become curable, the stigma lingered and survivors would be outcast. The project was run a team of incredibly devoted people but they had extremely limited funding.

Something happened to my mum when she went to Sanjay Nagar. It changed her. India changed her. A part of her soul came alive and she came back to the UK on a mission, speaking out about her experiences, fundraising for the project and committing to creating change. She unexpectedly died the following year, but the bridge that she had set up between the university and Sanjay Nagar had continued to be nourished, blossoming in incredible directions. It was now combined with *Snehalaya*, a larger project with many branches, including supporting sex workers. Each year, the university selected a group of students to fundraise and go and visit the project.

I was staring at the advert calling for the next group. I applied and was lovingly welcomed in. It felt very significant for us all. For the first time since her death when I was 13, I felt inexplicably close to my mum. The grief took on a different quality; it wasn't a hole anymore. I was with her.

India changed everything for me, too. As soon as I got there, something shifted. I felt a force of spirituality that I'd never experienced. The mystical was so alive and present, and every person I met knew it, relating consciously with it. We all co-existed in a shared field of connection with the invisible creative force that animates everything, silently nodding and smiling our knowing's to one another. I had no desire to drink or take drugs; I'd found spirituality. I discovered presence. I witnessed ritual and surrender and kindness and aliveness. I witnessed dead bodies burning and the sweetest prayer-filled scents filling the streets. I met people that had met and treasured my mum. I saw the lives that had changed because she existed. I sat in the building they'd named after her (The Catherine Pearson Memorial Building) and played with children. My grief opened and I finally felt able to allow it. And as the grief opened, so did my heart. I met Dr Hulbe, the project's founder and head of the local social work college, who had created huge waves of change in Ahmednagar throughout his life. I witnessed what it means to live a life which has impact. I was living the opposite of the self-destruct I'd been experiencing at home. The reverse of the meaningless culture I'd been raised within. I dropped out of university and stayed in India for six months until my visa ran out.

During that time, I relapsed once, shaved my head and had numerous heart - and mind - exploding experiences. One of these was meeting a man on a bus who was scattering his niece's ashes. We bonded over all the ways India was healing and transforming our grief. I told him about Sanjay Nagar and what I'd been doing. Our travelling paths wove together for a few weeks, but unbeknown to either of us, our meeting would change the course of his life and many other peoples, too. I later introduced him to the amazing woman co-ordinating and leading the student visits from the university, and after a few years, the two of them moved to India together, working full-time for Snehalaya. They're still there now, changing lives for the better every single day.

The following six years of my life were filled with trials and tribulations, growth, pain, beautiful people and lots of love. Though I'd taken the lid off the grief, the wounds of having and losing such a remarkable woman as a mum are complicated. I continued to process following the thawing out of my ability to feel. But the call to kids still echoed in my being. It's such a profound and weird thing, this calling. I don't know how it came into being, but my spirit won't stop pushing me with it. Everything always leads me back here.

I decided to return to university to finish my degree. I wanted to be taken seriously. I wanted to change things. And I felt I needed academic proof of my validity to make it happen. I was met by the same tutors that had taught me previously and I'm not sure where

I'd be without those people. They were such beacons of light and inspiration. The commitment they had and have to children's rights was profoundly inspirational and translated into deeply supportive relationships with us students, too. I graduated with a first-class honours, after writing a thesis which examined adventure playgrounds from a radical Feminism perspective.

Following my degree, I returned to living and working as a therapist, intuitive channel, energy worker and astrologer. My passion for kids still engulfed me when I let it, but I couldn't find a place where I could show up as myself. I'd received initiations from incredible teachers and powerful places on the planet and become a recognised voice of the galactic Mayan calendar. I was living as my stellar-obsessed, dimension-bending, ceremony-creating soul self and I couldn't bear to be in spaces where I had to hide that. I couldn't find a place that let my heart, soul and devotion to kids breathe all at once.

I searched and searched for a way I could work with young people but everywhere I looked my soul screamed, "NO!" I had non-negotiables now. I would not embody an abusive power dynamic, I would not detach from my soul and I would not force-feed children information. Then I found Steiner education. For a while, I felt I'd found my place. Collaborating with people that led deeply spiritual lives and were devoted, heart and soul, to children. And the children set my being alight; being around them was everything! But it was still a forced learning environment and eventually I couldn't handle it. The more I went through the training and dug into anthroposophy, the more it didn't feel right for me. The road called me again and I was led to Australia.

I landed for a month in the Blue Mountains, a sacred Aboriginal location and a potent spot for UFO sightings. I was volunteering with a group of 15 incredible people at a retreat centre. My time there was profound in lots of ways. Mainly because of the land. It felt bogglingly familiar and I wanted to live there forever, a feeling I've not really had anywhere else on the planet. And the people were so indie and alternative. Not in an Instagram way, but in a late 90s skate culture, Deftones and Incubus way. It felt like home galactically, as a Gaia devotee and as a little mosher kid, too! I feel now that it was because it was a sacred spot for my destiny...

One day I was in the local town, picking lavender from a huge bush in the street. I had a lovely chat with an old lady that was doing the same and took a turn down a road I'd not explored before. There I stumbled into a tiny library - if you've not gathered by now, I truly love books. I immediately started smile-crying as I saw a little poster with an arrow to the exhibition that was currently being showed. An exhibition about children's play.

As I wandered around the hilarious displays and installations, my heart began sparkling again. I couldn't believe what I was being confronted by. I came out of the exhibition fully charged and was met by a shelf filled with playwork books. Playwork as a field is relatively tiny. I'd never seen our books anywhere other than the university library. I sobbed my heart out and got the message straight away. I was being guided back to academia.

You know this bit of the story - the desire to study Summerhill, the discovery of their whopping fees and the redirect to charter schooling in the States, whilst living in Goa for the season. The scheduled dates for my visit to California aligned somewhat with a conference about play, taking place in West Virginia. My tutor amongst a few others from the university were attending and encouraged me to apply to speak about my research. I soon found myself in the Deep South for an academic conference after having not worn shoes for six months and living far, far removed from traditional society.

This is when the wheels of my education journey, unsurprisingly, fell off (again).

I learned several things from that conference. Firstly, I didn't fit and had no desire to make myself fit into the academic community. Though my talk went really well, I'd gone from tantric eye-gazing workshops to ironed suits and hard chairs, from tearful sharing circles of equality to a hierarchical institution where the letters you had behind your name and the staff you had under you mattered. There were some potent insights presented and no doubt there were also lots of interesting people, but the whole environment felt painful to me. And it bruised my little soul. I'd been opened so much by Mama Oz and Mama India and the whole situation felt… spikey. Though there were references to some cool projects supporting young people, a lot of the research seemed to just be echoing within the academic community. My heart and soul were eager for social change, and in that moment, if I'm honest, I realised that submission of a thesis would not create impact.

When I landed with the schools and started my research, though, I felt it again. That synchronistic, heart throbbing, explosive, 'this is exactly where you're meant to be' feeling. Within both schools, in different ways, I found home again. I was moved beyond anything I'd ever experienced. I saw all I had studied and dreamed of actualised. I witnessed that it is possible, that it is being lived, and if it exists there, it can exist anywhere. Enriching, inspiring, consented opportunities for kids with space for them to be in charge of themselves and navigate relationships consciously, facilitated by people that could really see them. The young people

I met were incredible, changing and activating parts of me that continue to glow because of their touch.

I got back to the UK in such conflict. The inspiration had almost dislodged my heart, it was so big. But I couldn't see how I could continue within academia. I didn't believe that my research could translate into social action. And if it didn't, what was the point? I wanted to show the world what I'd seen, but my thesis wouldn't be seen by anyone. I met a beautiful man, fell deeply in love and though I'd had the most heart-opening, inspiring experience with the schools I'd visited, I dropped out of university again, felt like a failure and painfully closed off that aspect of my being.

Fast forward a year or two... Covid is a thing and I'm back in my hometown of Bradford, searching for a place to live in order to be close to my grandfather for the remaining months of his life. I'm temporarily staying at the coolest Airbnb you've ever seen. A little art den of creative wonder, with an actual swing in the kitchen! I am re-finding myself following a life-changing relationship and difficult breakup, which put lots of things into perspective. Crawling up to the little cubby-hole mezzanine bed for the first time, I browse the bookshelf and almost fall off the edge. Again, I am confronted by books I've only ever seen in the university library (thank you, Ivan Illich) and the soul itch that NOTHING has come close to subduing gets turned UP.

I didn't feel inspired, though. I felt sad. Really sad. The deepest soul grief I've felt bubbled up to the surface and I sobbed all night. I couldn't even look at the books. I turned the other way. How could it be that something that had moved me so deeply and literally guided my life had led to a dead end? I shook my first at Spirit. But even in my tantrum, I felt the synchronicity and knew there was something there. I decided to contact the woman who owned the Airbnb and organised to go for a coffee.

The meeting was mega. I learned that she was an author; a remarkable, unique and inspiring woman. I told her why the books had touched me so much and of my research. We had many parallels. She had dropped out of her MPhil to return years later after people prodded her to realise that her research was important. She told me that I needed to share my work with the world. During our conversation, I realised that I also wanted to. It was my deepest desire. But I couldn't and wouldn't disconnect from my soul to make it happen. And I most certainly didn't want to pursue it through the echo chamber of academia. She suggested I wrote a book.

It has been 20 months since that meeting. I watched my grandfather, a man I loved deeply, descend as death embraced him. I have no idea how but I've done it. I've written the book. I turned 30 as I completed my writing and there's something that feels poignant about that. Goodness knows how many hours I've poured into these pages, but I tell you what, it's the most fulfilling thing I've ever done. Everything you've read has been alive inside of me, wanting to burst from the seams of my soul, and now it's outside, birthed so that people like you can access it.

If you want to keep an eye on what I'm up to, I'm on social media channels @jyotiimix and my website is www.jyotiimix.com.

Oh, and one final note...

I recently learned that the Catherine Pearson Memorial Building at Sanjay Nagar was knocked down to make space for a series of apartment blocks. Thanks to Snehalaya and the two amazing humans mentioned, every person in the slum community was gifted an apartment, for free, built specifically for them.

The seeds we plant might not grow in our lifetime, but someone else might just come along and look after them until they bloom.

I ask you again, dear human: what are *you* gonna do about school?

ACE STUFF I READ/WATCHED

I recommend these:

Books

Akala (2019): Natives: Race and Class in the Ruins of Empire

Fraser Brown and others (2008): Foundations of Playwork

Julia Cameron (1992): The Artist's Way: A Course in Discovering and Recovering Your Creative Self

Paulo Freire (1968): Pedagogy of the Oppressed

Tim Gill (2007): No Fear: Growing Up in a Risk Averse Society

Peter Gray (2013): Free to Learn: Why Unleashing the Instinct to Play Will Make Our Children Happier, More Self-Reliant, and Better Students for Life

Kent Hoffman (2016): Raising a Secure Child: How Circle of Security Parenting Can Help You Nurture Your Child's Attachment, Emotional Resilience, and Freedom to Explore

John Holt (1964): How Children Fail

Aldous Huxley (1932): A Brave New World

Aldous Huxley (1954): Doors of Perception

Ivan Illich (1971): Deschooling Society

Jiddu Krishnamurti (1969): Freedom from the Known

Grace Llewellyn (1991): The Teenage Liberation Handbook: How to Quit School and Get a Real Life and Education

Alexander Sutherland Neill (1960): Summerhill: A Radical Approach to Child Rearing

Sue Palmer (2007): Toxic Childhood: How the Modern World is Damaging our Children and What We Can Do About It

Ken Robinson (2009): The Element: How Finding Your Passion Changes Everything

Juno Roche (2019): Trans Power: Own Your Gender

Marshall Rosenberg (1999): Nonviolent Communication - A Language of Life: Life-Changing Tools for Healthy Relationships

Colin Ward (1978): The Child in the City

UN Convention on the Rights of the Child (1992) : access via ipaworld.org

Playwork Principles Scrutiny Group (2005): The Playwork Principles : access via playwales.org

Documentaries

Channel 4 (2015): Sex in Class

Erin Davis (2015): The Land: An Adventure Play Documentary

Magnolia Pictures (2013): Black Fish

Ken Robinson (2006): TED Talk: Do Schools Kill Creativity?

Websites

Agile Learning Centres: www.agilelearningcenters.org

The Alliance for Self-Directed Education: www.self-directed.org

International Play Association: www.ipaworld.org

Flying Squads: Where Youth Rights Take Flight: www.flyingsquads.org

Snehalaya: Women's Empowerment: www.snehalaya.org

More books (if you wanna geek out):

Children's Rights: Politics & Sociology

Phillipe Aries (1962): Centuries of Childhood

Pierre Bourdieu (1984): Distinction: A Social Critique of the Judgement of Taste

Pierre Bourdieu (1986): The Forms of Capital in Handbook of Theory and Research for the Sociology of Education

Emily Charkin (2014): A Parable of the Way Things Ought to Be in Education, Childhood and Anarchism: Talking Colin Ward

Carl Cohen (1971): Democracy

Joe Feagin (1984): Racial & Ethnic Relations

Michel Foucault (1972): The Archaeology of Knowledge

Sharon Gewirtz and Alan Cribb (2002): Plural Conceptions of Social Justice: Implications for Policy Sociology

Barry Golson (2001): The Demonization of Children in Children in Society: Contemporary Theory, Policy and Practice

Karl Hanson (2017): Embracing the Past: 'Been', 'Being' and 'Becoming' Children in Childhood

John Holt (1974): Escape from Childhood

Derek Hook (2007): Foucault, Psychology and the Analytics of Power

Allison James (2009): Agency in The Palgrave Handbook of Childhood Studies

Allison James & Adrian James (2004): Constructing Childhood Theory, Policy and Social Practice

Allison James & Adrian James (2008): Key Concepts in Childhood Studies

Allison James & Alan Prout (1997): Constructing and Reconstructing Childhood: Contemporary Issues in the Sociological Study of Childhood

Marc Jans (2004): Children as Citizens: Towards a Contemporary Notion of Child Participation

Chris Jenks (1996): Childhood

Nick Lee (2001): Childhood and Society: Growing Up in an Age of Uncertainty

Berry Mayall (2002): Towards a Sociology for Childhood: Thinking from Children's Lives

Jens Qvortrup (2004): The Waiting Child

Matt Qvortrup (1994): Childhood Matters: Social Theory, Practice and Politics

Madan Sarup (1983): Marxism/Structuralism/Education: Theoretical Developments in the Sociology of Education

Karen Seccombe (1999): "So You Think I Drive a Cadillac?" Welfare Recipients' Perspectives on the System and Its Reform

Anne Solberg (2005): Negotiating Childhood in Constructing and Reconstructing Childhood

Emma Uprichard (2008): Children as 'Being and Becomings': Children, Childhood and Temporality in Children & Society

Mike Wragg (2011): The Child's Right to Play: Rhetoric or Reality in Children's Rights in Practice

Mike Wragg (2018): The Neoliberalisation of Childhood and the Future of Playwork in Aspects of Playwork in Play and Culture Studies

Child-Centric Practice

Fraser Brown (2018) Aspects of Playwork in Play and Culture Studies

Jan Fook & Fiona Gardner (2007): Practicing Critical Reflection

Bob Hughes (2001): Evolutionary Playwork

Stuart Lester (2018) Playwork & the Cocreation of Play Spaces: The Rhythms and Refrains of a Play Environment in Aspects of Playwork in Play and Culture Studies

Ramesh Manocha (2017): Nurturing Young Minds: Mental Wellbeing in the Digital Age

Stephanie Schim & Ardith Doorenbos (2001): A Three-dimensional Model of Cultural Congruence: Framework for Intervention

Education

John Dewey (1916): Democracy and Education

Michael Fielding (2014): Bringing freedom to education: Colin Ward, Alex Bloom and the Possibility of Radical Democratic Schools in Education, Childhood and Anarchism: Talking Colin Ward

Daniel Greenberg (1987): Free at Last: The Sudbury Valley School Book

Tomas Boronski & Nasima Hassan (2015) Sociology of Education

Jackie Kilvington & Ali Wood (2018): Reflective Playwork

Barry Down, John Smyth. & Peter McInerney (2014): The Socially Just School: Making Space for Youth to Speak Back

Maria Montessori (1912): The Montessori Method

Heather Piper & Ian Stronach (2009): Summerhill - The Touching Example of Summerhill School in Alternative Education for the 21st Century

Claire Pugh, Dave Bullough & Ben Tawil (2018): The Land in Aspects of Playwork in Play and Culture Studies

Trond Solhaug (2018): Democratic Schools – Analytical Perspectives in Journal of Social Science Education

Glenys Woods & Philip Woods (2009): Alternative Education for the 21st Century: Philosophies, Approaches, Visions

John Smyth & Terry Wrigley (2013): Living on the Edge: Re-thinking Poverty, Class and Schooling

Play

Gordon Burghardt (2005): The Genesis of Animal Play: Testing the Limits

William Cosaro (2003): We're Friends Right? Inside Kids Culture

Sylwyn Guilbaud (2018): The Might of Play as Possibility and Power in Aspects of Playwork in Play and Culture Studies

Pentti Hakarrainen (1999): Play & Motivation in Perspectives in Activity Theory

Jack Halberstam (2011) The Queer Art of Failure

Ali Wood and Jacky Kilvington (2016): Gender, Sex and Children's Play

Sacha Powell & Ian Wellard (2008): Policies & Play: The Impact of National Policies on Children's Opportunities for Play

Emily Ryall, Wendy Russell and Malcolm MacLean (2013): The Philosophy of Play

Roger Smith (2010): A Universal Child?

William Sumner (1979): Folkways and Mores

Brian Sutton-Smith (1997): The Ambiguity of Play

Kathy Sylva (1982): Child Development: A First Course

Science

David Bohm (1951): Quantum Theory

David Bohm & Jiddu Krishnamurti (1985): The Ending of Time

Steiner

Josh Dunning (2020): Biodynamics' Dirty Secret: Ecofascism, Karmic Racism and the Nazis

Martyn Rawson and Tobias Richter (2000): Educational Tasks and Content of the Steiner Waldorf Curriculum

Rudolf Steiner (1922): The Education of the Child in the Light of Anthroposophy

He has achieved success who has lived well, laughed often, and loved much;
Who has enjoyed the trust of pure women, the respect of intelligent men and the love of little children;
Who has filled his niche and accomplished his task;
Who has never lacked appreciation of Earth's beauty or failed to express it;
Who has left the world better than he found it,
Whether an improved poppy, a perfect poem, or a rescued soul;
Who has always looked for the best in others and given them the best he had;
Whose life was an inspiration;
Whose memory a benediction.

Bessie Anderson Stanley

(Often incorrectly quoted as Ralph Waldo Emmerson)